IT'S NEVER TOO LATE: 150 Men and Women Who Changed Their Careers

Robert K. Otterbourg

BARRON'S

DEDICATION

To Samuel Weaver Otterbourg and the wonders of his twenty-first century career.

All inquiries should be addressed to:
Barron's Educational Series, Inc.
250 Wireless Boulevard
Hauppauge, New York 11788

Library of Congress Catalog Card No. 92-34938
International Standard Book No. 0–8120–1464–2

Library of Congress Cataloging-in-Publication Data

Otterbourg, Robert K.
    It's never too late : 150 men and women who changed their careers / by Robert K. Otterbourg.
        p.   cm.
    ISBN 0-8120-1464-2
    1. Career changes—United States—Case studies. I. Title.
HF5384.087   1993
650.14'0973—dc20   92-34938
                                                          CIP

PRINTED IN THE UNITED STATES

2 3 4 5 5 1 0 0 9 8 7 6 5 4 3 2 1

Contents

Preface   vii

How and Why They Did It   1

Chapter 1.   Why Change Careers?   3

Defining Career Changing   3
Selecting a New Career   4
Career Changing Through the Ages   5
Career Changers Are All Around Us   7
No, You're Not a "Kook"   8
Why the Rush, Anyway?   8
Getting the House in Order   9
The Multitalented   11
Once a Legal Secretary but Not Always   12
Career Changers Have Many Options   13

Chapter 2.   The Pink Slip Arrives   15

What's the Next Step?   15
The News Comes in the Form of Early Retirement   19
When Your Career Is Stonewalled   20

Chapter 3.   How Do I Know When I'm Ready?   22

Overcoming Inertia   22
Acting Upon a Dream   23
Take a Good Look in the Mirror   24
What Happens When You're Bored?   25
The Entrepreneurial Urge   26
"When the Cause It Is Just..."   28
Reflections in the Glass Ceiling   29

Chapter 4. Planning a Career Change 32

Career Assessment 32
Gathering the Facts 34
Attend Career Workshops 34
Exploring the Market 35
Furthering Your Education 36
The Need to Cut Costs 38

Chapter 5. The Art of Piggybacking 41

Base Your Career Change on Experience 41
Borrowing from the Past 44

Chapter 6. Finding a New Lifestyle 48

How Career Changers Define Lifestyle 49
How Important Is Location? 50
There's More to Life Than Money 52
Lifestyle Is in Flux in the Corporate World 53
The Home Office Comes of Age 54

Chapter 7. The Hobbyist Goes to Work 57

Chapter 8. Hanging up the Uniform 63

The Military 63
The Challenge 63
Into the Classrooms 66
Police and Firefighters 67

And Those Who Have Done It 71

Chapter 9. Education 73

Chapter 10. Health Care 89

Career Opportunities as a Doctor 89
Career Opportunities as a Nurse 105

Chapter 11. Law 110

Chapter 12. Clergy 124

Chapter 13. Community Service and Psychological Services 139

Career Opportunities in Community Service 139
Career Opportunities in Psychological Services 147

Career 14. Retail and Service Businesses 152

Career Opportunities in Retailing 152
Career Opportunities in Bookselling 157
Career Opportunities in Bed-and-Breakfast Inns 161
Career Opportunities as a Cook and Restauranteur 163

Chapter 15. Home Improvement and Decor 169

Chapter 16. Gardening, Farming, and the Environment 177

Career Opportunities in Gardening 177
Career Opportunities in Farming 179
Career Opportunities in the Environment 184

Chapter 17. Communications and the Arts 188

Career Opportunities in Writing and Journalism 188
Career Opportunities in Public Relations 192
Career Opportunities in Art and Acting 195

Notes 202

Bibliography 205

Resources 206

Acknowledgments

It's Never Too Late was written to help others explore and better understand the many possibilities in changing careers. To some extent, it reflects my own search. In the process of writing this book, I learned a lot about myself. I hope readers benefit in the same way.

I owe a particular debt of gratitude to the 150 career changers who were interviewed. They shared their dreams as well as their doubts on career changing.

A few people stand out. William Zimmerman, a long-time friend and a *Newsday* editor, encouraged me to take an article I wrote for his newspaper and develop it into a book.

Susan Lawley, a one-time Goldman Sachs & Company vice president, typifies the spirit of the many people who assisted me over the past year. A career changer herself, Susan cheerfully answered my questions and then suggested a number of career changers I might interview.

Special appreciation goes to Patricia Burton for proofreading the manuscript and recommending structural changes. My literary agent, Edward Knappman of New England Publishing Associates, furnished sound counsel and reliable editorial advice, and Lynn Griffo Sackman, my editor at Barron's, furnished constructive editorial assistance throughout this project.

And last, a hearty thanks to my family for patiently sharing my enthusiasm for this project, especially to my wife, Susan, who listened to my collection of anecdotes, up to and including our evening "pillow talk."

Robert K. Otterbourg

Preface

If you're in your early thirties to midfifties this book is written for you.

It's Never Too Late is a book about career changers, approximately 150 men and women from all walks of life who switched careers. By telling their stories, *It's Never Too Late* will encourage and guide others also to change careers.

The diverse cast of characters in *It's Never Too Late* has much in common. They have all taken greater charge of their lives. In doing so, they were willing to assume financial, professional, and personal risk, best summarized by an anonymous author's comment: "No matter how many loving hands may be stretched out to help us, some paths were tread alone."

I deliberately avoided a Noah's ark approach in selecting career changers. My sole criterion was whether the individuals had an interesting story to tell. I also discovered an absence of regional characteristics in career changing. The personal and occupational challenges are the same in San Francisco, Chicago, Atlanta, and Boston.

Career changers are alike in other ways. Most showed a willingness to set aside rank and title to start their new careers, often on the bottom run of the ladder. If this wasn't sufficient challenge, they reported to men and women 10 to 25 years younger.

Career changing is accelerating as a result of different economic and social factors that are rocking our society. More than any other factors, the twin effects of corporate downsizing and early retirement are helping to enlarge the pool of career changers.

Career switching also calls for reevaluation of personal and family resources. Some career changers dipped into savings, were supported by spouses, reduced their material needs, or used the proceeds from the sale of a business to make the switch financially feasible.

The contents sets the stage: Chapters 1 through 8 establish the trends. They show the factors that cause people to change careers. Chapters 9 through 17 present a series of different careers, contain how-to information about career changing, and tell the stories of the people who have made career changes.

Don't be disappointed if you fail to find a specific career. This book does not intend to be encyclopedic. It offers readers a panorama of many different career-changing options. The people you meet in every chapter have stories to tell that are similar to your own.

I'm continually asked if career changers are happy in their new work. Without defining "happiness," my answer is an unqualified "yes." Perhaps the question was best answered in *Hamlet* when Polonius advised his son, "this above all: to thine own self be true."

HOW AND WHY
THEY DID IT

Before deciding to change careers, it is necessary to understand what's taking place in the employment market, specifically in corporate America. Chapters 1 through 8 evaluate the important trends and dynamics of career changing in the 1990s.

Career changers must know how, why, and when to change careers. What do you do when the pink slip arrives, and how do you apply previous skills or hobbies to a new career? Some career changers planned their move years in advance; they had the luxury of time. Others, however, had to make their decision literally over a weekend.

The first eight chapters contain more than theory. Anecdotal examples and profiles also provide insight on why there is an acceleration in career changing today.

Why Change Careers?

Thanks to Carl, I learned a valuable lesson in career changing. My education took place the day after my computer malfunctioned. This occurred at a critical phase in writing this book, and I thought I was out of business. My computer problem was fortunately solved in a few hours.

I was having lunch at the counter of a local restaurant, and the man to my left and I started to talk. "How's it going?" he asked. "Better than yesterday, when my computer went down," I answered. He was curious about why the computer was so vital to my work.

After I told him about my book on career changing, he said, "My name's Carl and I'm a career changer. We just sold our family beauty supply business and I got a new career. I'm selling jewelry. I guess if I'm lucky I'll change careers only once or twice more."

Contrary to Carl's definition, job changing is not career changing. Some of us hold 8 to 10 different *jobs* over a 40-year period yet these changes can hardly be classified as career switching. Like Carl's, they are usually variations of the same theme.

DEFINING CAREER CHANGING

Is career changing as simple as Carl's description, or does it involve other considerations? *It's Never Too Late* examines this question in the next eight chapters. Before you're ready to change careers, you should examine a number of key social, economic, psychological, and human interest factors.

We need to know how lifestyle affects career change and how to use hobbies or piggyback existing skills in another career. Also, what is the best way to prepare for change, and above all, how do you know when you're ready for the move?

The formula for career changing is rather basic: if the entrance requirements are demanding—in terms of investing in a business, attending professional school, learning a new skill, or being certified or licensed to work in the field—chances are career switching will occur infrequently, perhaps only once or twice in a lifetime. When there is ease of entrance, more career changes can be expected.

Career changing means different things to different people. There's one set of guidelines for managers, professionals, and technicians and another for semiskilled workers.

As head of an undergraduate humanities program at Davidson College in North Carolina, Rosemary Tong defines career changing in the language of the 1990s. Dr. Tong's comments are directed toward premed students, but her remarks are usually applicable to most occupations. She found that career changing even among medical doctors is becoming a regular occurrence, and she encourages premed students to prepare realistically for the future. "During their professional careers, they'll wear several hats. Careers are starting to come into existence that we never thought about earlier." [1]

SELECTING A NEW CAREER

As children we were asked, What do we want to do when we grow up? This was a serious question because it was assumed that selecting a career was a permanent decision. This is no longer the case.

The willingness to switch careers is actually consistent with what is taking place in most other parts of our lives. We have become peripatetic. We jet here and jet there. We start one college but graduate from another. We dispose of products rather than repair them. We lease cars to avoid a long-term commitment, and tragically, we even marry with the same attitude.

Call it what you like, it's all part of the "you only go around once" theory. Tom Sawyer maintained that "work consists of whatever a body is obliged to do, and that play consists of whatever a body is not obliged to do."

Our attitudes toward career changing are different from attitudes of a decade ago. We're no longer content to work for a single employer until we're eligible to collect a pension. At the same time, we've been cajoled into believing that the retirement years are the best years, and in some ways the statistics support these claims.

Since 1930, life expectancy has increased nearly 15 years, to age 75. Although the American Association of Retired Persons starts recruiting members at 50, few people feel old at that age, or at 60. The 55 year old looks forward to changing careers as readily as a man or woman 20 years younger.

There are many reasons for the accelerated interest in career changing, some intellectual, some economic, and some emotional. Corporate downsizing continues to be a critical factor fueling career changing. Over an 11-year period from 1980 through 1991, employment at *Fortune* 500 companies shrunk from 16 to 12 million. Those who lose their jobs become candidates for career change, and those remaining with the company feel uncertain about future employment.

Middle management, according to the American Management Association, is picking up the brunt of corporate downsizing. Middle managers comprise about 5 to 8 percent of the work force, but they represented nearly 17 percent of those discharged during 1991. Downsizing affected professional, technical, and supervisory personnel equally hard, with job losses among these employees at nearly 23 percent of the discharged work force.

Downsizing has helped accelerate the search for career alternatives. There's a 1990s quest for a more simple life, or as *Time Magazine* put it, "Goodbye to having it all. Tired of trendiness and materialism, Americans are rediscovering the joys of home life, basic values and the things that last."

Work force shrinkage and the disappearance of many middle-management jobs have drastically shortened the multirun ladders of career paths once prevalent in large corporations. The Conference Board noted in a 1991 study that employees can no longer "count on a lifelong succession of improving job opportunities provided by a single employer. Implicit in these changes is the expectation that employees must assume greater responsibility for managing their own careers to prepare for the volatile conditions ahead." [2]

Even among those unaffected by downsizing, a recurring question is, Do I want to do the same work for the next 10 to 20 years?

CAREER CHANGING THROUGH THE AGES

In an era when we do something once and it is considered a special event, and when it is repeated it becomes a significant social trend, career changing is a trend. What is unique about the 1990s is the current intensity in career switching, a point to be examined in the next several chapters.

To be precise, career switching in its broadest sense has roots in U.S. history. George Washington, the classic career changer, was a farmer, surveyor, soldier, and statesman. Thomas Jefferson had an even more diversified career as a lawyer, farmer, author, architect, diplomat, and statesman.

Earlier in this century, Albert Schweitzer personified the diverse range of career changing. At age 38, Schweitzer, a Protestant theologian and a classically trained organist, became a doctor. He then spent the next 50 years running a mission hospital in central Africa, funding it through book royalties and organ concerts.

The stimulus to write this book is contemporary, however. In 1988, after 20 years in the public relations field, I decided to change careers. I considered different options. Instead of making a more radical change to a new field, I made an easy transition from publicist to writer—hardly a daring change but sufficient to pique my curiosity. How many other people are changing careers? Until then, my family, friends, and business associates had rather consistent careers.

When I started my research in mid-1989, A. Bartlett Giamatti, professor of medieval literature at Yale University and subsequently its president, was listed high on my list of prospective candidates to profile in this book.

Giamatti, the quintessential career changer, fulfilled his lifetime passion for baseball when he was named commissioner of the National League and then commissioner of baseball. Unfortunately we never met. He died in September 1989 before an interview could be scheduled. What initially attracted me to Giamatti was a *Sports Illustrated* article:

"Being president of a university is no way for an adult to make a living. Sir, is being commissioner of baseball, likewise, any way for a grown-up to spend his waking hours? Yes, an adult should be commissioner, because in any adult will always lurk a child, and if you don't try to find an adult for the job, the child will simply take over. You've got to watch that."[3]

What distinguished Giamatti's career pattern is that he knew how to switch careers, forge ahead into a new career, and employ lessons learned in the past to enrich his new work.

CAREER CHANGERS ARE ALL AROUND US

It's Never Too Late is not about superheroes. Except for author Tom Clancy and TV anchor Catherine Crier, none of the other career switchers mentioned or profiled in this book are household names. Rather than a catalog of the "rich and famous," the lives portrayed are in many ways representative of 45 million U.S. men and women aged 35 to 54 years, or 42 percent of the current work force, who are potential career changers.

Career switchers are all around us. Networking produced many of my interviews. Nearly 40 percent of the people I interviewed were found by word of mouth. Friends, and friends of friends, suggested candidates. People I interviewed knew other career changers.

The soil is rich. Dig up the top layer and you find career changers. My approach is one that you can use in your own career. Even if you feel that you know few career changers personally, you'll soon find that a little digging will produce a list of candidates. Speak with them. They'll share with you, as they did with me, their experiences.

When I was having my annual medical exam, the doctor, Steven Cohen, suggested I interview both his wife, Sally, now an internist who did not enter medical school until her late 30s, and his uncle, Norman Tanenbaum, who became a lawyer while also in his late 30s. Sally in turn recommended Murray Hulse, a one-time insurance company executive turned carpenter, who custom built several pieces of furniture in the Cohen home.

Philip Adelman and I are fellow trustees of the Flat Rock Nature Association in Englewood, New Jersey. Phil told me that he had sold his office supply business and was attending law school. He suggested that I interview his wife, Ruth, who became a nurse in her late 30s.

Networking also brought me in touch with Pat Monroe, a former tennis partner, client, and corporate marketer, who moved from Ridgewood, New Jersey to Manchester Center, Vermont in search of a better lifestyle and to buy a retail store. Pat passed me along to a fellow Manchester Center resident, Ed Morrow, who left Wall Street in the 1970s to become a bookseller.

And little did I know when I called a former next-door neighbor in Ridgewood, Ron Dooley, now living in Calgary, to tell him that I had become a grandfather, that he would suggest his boyhood friend, Jim Marshall. Jim is a one-time printer who now designs and builds artistic brick walls in Medicine Hat, Alberta.

I found Barry Rein, a chemist and former corporate marketing executive, when I stayed at his bed-and-breakfast inn in Cape May, New Jersey. Also as a result of networking, I met Leah Richter when I was sitting at the swimming pool that serves our homeowner's association. Leah, a one-time science teacher and dental supply company executive, was busily reviewing her law school lecture notes.

NO, YOU'RE NOT A "KOOK"

I asked one former client if he could suggest any friends or associates who were career changers for inclusion in this book. During our talk, he described career changers as "quitters," a view somewhat contradictory to Ralph Waldo Emerson's commentary that "a foolish consistency is the hobgoblin of little minds."

Others denigrate career switchers as "loose cannons" or "kooks." When Nechama Goldberg (late thirties), a textile marketing executive and corporate strategist, announced that she would be leaving her high-paying marketing job for what she considered greater opportunities as a rabbi, her boss was disappointed that a "rising star could spurn advancement and opportunities." Coworkers failed to understand how she could leave now that she was on the fast track after so many years of struggle.

Wick & Company, a research firm, found similar reactions when it studied the reasons that women leave corporate jobs. They learned that men, more than women, feared that they would be perceived as "flighty." Men it was discovered, felt more trapped in unsatisfying jobs because their role models often spent a lifetime at the same company. In comparison, women do not settle as readily as men for dead-end jobs.

WHY THE RUSH, ANYWAY?

It doesn't take too long to discover why so many of us are switching careers. Whether they were downsized or left their jobs voluntarily, most of the people profiled in this book "wanted to do their own thing."

Psychologists and behavioral scientists have a field day telling us about the inner motivations behind career changing. There's even an increase in the level of daydreaming among midlife executives, Judith Meyerowitz noted in her doctoral thesis. Those who are satisfied with their work normally do not daydream, but most other workers between 35 and 54 shift from thinking about their present work and fantasize about possible future jobs. The daydreamer starts asking, Is this how I really want to spend the rest of my business life?

By comparison, enthusiasm is rampant among corporate high achievers, says author Gail Sheehy. Surveying graduates of the Harvard Business School, she learned that "the happiest were presidents and the unhappiest were vice presidents ... two-thirds of the unhappiest men said that they would love to change what they do—but they don't."

An advertising executive told Sheehy that "most people, if they haven't made it by 45, begin to coast. They just want to get to the end without making any mistakes." When she asked him if he had ever considered quitting and starting a new career, the adman said that he was too lazy, he had too soft a job. "I had nothing to do—just supervise other people. I was too well paid and had too many comforts to let go."

Sheehy's mentor, Daniel Levinson, best known for his analysis of the midlife crisis, notes that during a man's thirties he starts to recognize that his career will fall short of his earlier dreams.

"This is a crucial turning point. He may decide to continue in his present job, doing work that is increasingly routine and humiliating. He may change to another job or another occupation that offers more challenge and satisfaction. Or he may reduce his interest in work, performing well enough to keep employed but investing more in other aspects of life such as family or leisure."[4]

GETTING THE HOUSE IN ORDER

There is a growing interest for some people with otherwise successful careers to step off the fast track to get on what Leonard Schlesinger of the Harvard Business School calls the "sanity track." Both Peter Lynch (midforties) and his successor Morris Smith (midthirties) of the Fidelity Investments Magellan Fund followed Schlesinger's advice.

In May 1990, Lynch, who built the Magellan Fund over a 13-year period into the nation's largest mutual fund, quit so he could dedicate himself to philanthropy. Smith, as successful as Lynch as a money manager, resigned 23 months later since "there is more to life than money and management." Before making his next career move, he and his family are spending a year in Israel.

Lynch and Smith found their around-the-clock financial management responsibilities overwhelming, but other executives in high-pressure jobs seem to thrive on stressful schedules. Similarly, some managers have the temperament and skills to change careers more easily than others, a concept that concurs with some of Michael Maccoby's findings.

Dividing executives into three groups—the jungle fighter, the company man, and the gamesman—Maccoby indicates that these executives are mainly motivated by combinations of power, organization, and group dynamics.[5]

His fourth group is the craftsmen (lawyers, publicists, engineers, scientists, and technicians). "They want to do well and make money but are motivated more by solving problems, the intellectual challenge of the job, and the satisfaction in creating something of quality."

The craftsman, by temperament, training, experience, and career objective seems like the ideal candidate for career changing. As staff- and support-level executives, this group are also among the greatest casualties of corporate downsizing.

Even though mergers and acquisitions tend to eliminate redundant executive jobs, there have been relatively few converts among senior managers. Only occasionally do we hear of the chief executive officer of a large public company or a partner in a professional services firm who is switching careers. Yet Korn/Ferry International, an executive firm, found that 48 percent of senior executives interviewed said that if they had to do it all over again, they would select the same career, a considerable drop from the 60 percent level 10 years previously. In 1979, 17 percent of the surveyed executives planned to work as long as possible; a decade later this slipped to 10 percent.

George Gendron, editor of *Inc. Magazine*, confirms the rumblings of discontent in the executive suite. He found that half the entrepreneurial population is either on sabbatical or preparing to take one. Others are thinking about getting out of business altogether. They have reached the age when they start to question what they'll be doing with the rest of their lives.

I asked Bernard Goldstein, whose firm, Broadview Associates Inc. a merger and acquisition consultant in the computer services industry, why CEOs don't take the money and run after their company is acquired. I believed it was their chance to do something entirely different. Goldstein's succinct reply sums up the senior manager's plight: "Business is all they know."

THE MULTITALENTED

When senior managers switch careers, the maneuver is often subtle and within the accepted body language of the corporate boardroom. Different sets of escape routes are taken, ranging from accepting a high-level government appointment or heading up a nonprofit organization. Lawyers take another acceptable career-changing route within the profession by finding a new haven as a judge.

Other professionals and executives take a different path by combining several careers, an approach that goes far deeper than moonlighting on a second job. The additional career either enhances the existing career or is in a completely different field. In either instance, it meets the guidelines established by Susan Lawley, an outplacement consultant, who describes people who work proficiently in dual careers as "career blenders." (Her profile appears in Chapter 3.)

Louis Auchincloss (midseventies) has over the past 40 years combined two careers as a Wall Street corporate lawyer and a fiction writer. Lyle Greenfield (midforties) operates Bang Music, composers of commercials for radio and TV, and the Bridgehampton Winery on eastern Long Island. Other new career hybrids are growing in popularity, including physician–MBA, engineer–scientist–MBA, and nurse–lawyer, to the point that the American Association of Nurse Attorneys has grown since its founding in 1982 to over 640 members.

Then there's "going plural," which KPMG Career Consultancy Services defines as employing your skills, talents, and knowledge in a variety of different jobs simultaneously. Consistent with current downsizing trends, going plural provides a chance to "explore, marshall and channel all of your resources so that you can develop your future in the direction you want it to go."

The KPMG program is based on a concept advanced by Charles Handy, a London School of Economics professor, author, and TV broadcaster. In *The Age of Unreason*, he describes the need for a number of overlapping or "portfolio careers." Handy forecasts that the next generation of professionals, skilled technicians, and managers will start careers later, while in their mid- to late twenties, and leave earlier.

"By the time they are in their late forties or fifties they'll no longer want the pressure that the jobs will increasingly entail, but mainly because there will be younger more qualified and more energetic people available for these core jobs."

They'll move to another career or a series of careers, in keeping with Handy's definition of a portfolio career, which includes wage work and fee work, both forms of paid work; and home work, volunteer work, and study work, all forms of free work.

Handy set the tone with his own career portfolio, which consists of an annual schedule of 150 days of fee work, 50 days of volunteer work, 75 days of study, and 90 days of leisure.

ONCE A LEGAL SECRETARY BUT NOT ALWAYS

The title of the turn-of-the-century song, "Every Little Movement Has a Meaning All Its Own," could easily be the theme of Betsy Lazary Ern's (midthirties) career to date. Although they never met, Betsy could be one of Charles Handy's disciples. She has already created her version of a portfolio career as a consultant, author, and retailer.

Little in her past career or in growing up in Rochester, New York has been discarded. She retrieves and recycles experiences from the past in formulating her three-point career platform: "build on things of the past, life has its own plan so learn to roll with the punches, and don't be afraid to do new and different things."

Betsy, a New York State High School Regents scholar, wanted to study law, but as Betsy describes it, her parents lived in a world in which women didn't become lawyers. Instead she took a two-year college business course, moved to New York, and got a job with a large corporate law firm. As a legal secretary, she was described by some of the partners as "too smart for a secretary but not smart enough to be a paralegal professional."

By nature an entrepreneur, she left the law firm and utilized her office experiences as the basis to establish StepTakers, a consultancy retained by *Fortune* 500 companies to train secretaries and office administrators in how they can work more effectively in a corporate environment. Based on her previous careers as a consultant and secretary, she wrote *Good Bosses Do*, a how-to guide for secretaries and managers.

When her son Andrew was born, she moved StepTakers into her home to more easily accommodate work and family. Her experience operating an at-home business became the basis of *Don't Drop the Ball*, a book that tells other working mothers about her dual life.

As a teenager, Betsy enjoyed collecting dolls. Like many parts of her life, the memories were stored away. When her husband gave her a Barbie doll, the gift helped to incubate a hobby-related business, Memories in the Making, a retail store specializing in classic dolls and collectibles.

CAREER CHANGERS HAVE MANY OPTIONS

We have broadened our horizons to think in terms of *options*, a concept captured by Richard Ford in *The Sportswriter*. "A woman I met at the college where I briefly taught, once told me I had too many choices, that I was not driven enough by dire necessity. But this is just an illusion and her mistake. Choices are what we all need."[6]

Options give us the flexibility to be less rigid in evaluating new career paths. It provides an opportunity to relocate and create a new lifestyle or take a hobby and make it the basis of a new career.

Career changers enjoy other options. Change provides flexibility in starting a new career and even redirecting it when career objectives are not met, a situation that confronted George Latimer, Alfred Geduldig, and Sandy Lawrence. They left jobs with large organizations for new careers. Dissatisfied, they switched back to their earlier careers, but in the process they learned an important lesson: namely, you can return home.

When George Latimer (early sixties) was 47, he resigned as a captain in the New York City Transit Police and bought a chicken farm in Virginia. Ten years later, missing the excitement of police work and tired of chicken farming, he returned to New York as deputy chief of the Transit Police. (His profile appears in Chapter 16.)

Al Geduldig (midfifties) resigned as a vice president for public relations of a *Fortune* 500 company to live his dream of owning a restaurant. Poor timing and unfavorable business conditions in Rhode Island altered his plans, however. After a five-year struggle, he returned to public relations as vice president for public affairs of a major insurance company. (His profile appears in Chapter 17.)

Sandy Lawrence (midforties) was an up-and-comer when a corporate shuffle at the Gillette Company eliminated her job as vice president. Based on 16 years in consumer marketing at Gillette, several years with Xerox Corporation and an MBA, Sandy expected to find another executive job easily.

After reviewing various opportunities with an outplacement consultant, she took a gamble. With the help of investors she founded the Rose Garden, which represented a novel approach to selling quality, fresh roses at near wholesale price. Two stores were opened in Boston. Her business plan called for expanding to other cities.

"I went into business with the intention that it would have the potential for a salary equal to what I made at Gillette." Although the Rose Garden was operating on a break-even basis, Sandy's ambitious business plans were shaken by the recession.

Within a year of opening the first store, she realized that her temperament was better suited to the more structured lifestyle of a large company. It was time to reconsider her career options. Employing a full-time manager to run the Rose Garden, she joined Polaroid Corporation as vice president for worldwide consumer marketing.

---◆---

Points to Remember

► Career changing is not job changing.

► Corporate downsizing is taking its toll.

► Start networking if you want to meet career changers and hear their experiences.

► Career changing equates with "wanting to do my thing."

► Women do not want to stay employed in dead-end jobs.

► We can expect the pace of career changing to accelerate.

► A portfolio of careers represents one solution.

► Options provide flexibility in planning new careers.

---◆---

The Pink Slip Arrives

You're fired. These two words are some of the harshest in the English language. As both an employee and an employer, I know all too well the feeling these words inspire. However we try to dull its impact with euphemisms calling it "downsizing" or "realignment," the end result is the same: you're out of work and back in the job market.

WHAT'S THE NEXT STEP?

The usual route calls for updating a resumé and looking for a similar job with another organization in the same field. A somewhat bolder and riskier alternative is changing careers, an approach being taken with greater frequency by an undetermined number of downsized employees and early retirees.

Toni Heris (late fifties), a one-time advertising copywriter turned psychologist, counsels a number of career changers. Unless they have been fired, Toni finds that clients who have worked for large companies are less likely to switch careers. They often work for these companies to satisfy a need for security. Those in sales, advertising, and public relations, however, have a greater tendency to be gamblers.

Citing her own advertising career, she notes that "job security was never a factor, so I was risking very little when I changed careers and became a psychologist." (Her profile appears in Chapter 13.)

At this point, you most likely will be assigned for outplacement services. The American Management Association pointed out in its 1991 survey on downsizing and assistance to displaced employees that two-thirds of the companies reporting personnel reductions provided some form of outplacement assistance, and more than one-half of these firms did so for *all* of their discharged employees.

Downsized employees have more time to consider career alternatives, if the findings of Drake Beam Morin, Inc., an outplacement firm, are any indication. It now takes over 7 months to find a new job, compared with 5.2 months 3 years ago.[1] When downsized employees do get a new job, it is usually for less money than before. Even those executives receiving plump golden parachute settlements are shocked, angered, and depressed by being fired and are more hostile than ever toward their former employers.

Hostility aside, most downsized employees find new work in a similar field using their existing skills. A growing minority are seeking career alternatives, however: training for new professions or buying or starting a business, or in the case of some early retirees, they elect to build new careers based on Charles Handy's portfolio careers.

Becoming an entrepreneur seems to be catching on. Outplacement firms indicate that more downsized employees are inquiring about ways to train for a new profession or how to buy or start a business. At some offices of the outplacement consultants Lee Hecht Harrison, Inc., about 20 percent of the new clients seek information on self-employment.[2]

Many others, especially those 50 and older, become consultants. This sounds sensible, a good way to use existing skills and, above all, be your own boss. This is hardly the case, however. Few consultancies survive the first year on this formula. Unless your income goals are modest or you want to work on only a part-time basis, being a consultant for most career changers is an interlude in the career-changing process.

Get Ready in Advance

Some managers don't wait for the pink slip. They get ready for possible downsizing or early retirement. They prepare a personalized emergency or disaster plan; some even implement parts of the plan before being downsized.

Even though he was not fired from his bank job, Tom Wallis (midforties) contends that everyone should prepare a contingency plan. "If I have to do something else, what will it be? If I lose my job, what directions will I take?

After 18 years as a bank officer and branch manager in Arizona, Tom took his own advice. He initiated his "what-if" plan two years before he resigned from the bank by investigating opportunities in commercial photography. He read how-to books, and on a vacation he traveled from Phoenix to Santa Barbara, California to take a course on operating a commercial photography business. All the while, Tom was increasing his photographic skills.

When the time was ready—the twentieth anniversary of his joining the bank—Tom voluntarily resigned to become a commercial photographer.

A Tour with an Outplacement Firm

I met William Zimmerman (late forties) in the mid-1960s when Bill was a reporter with the *American Banker*, a daily banking newspaper. We remained friends as Bill's career progressed from reporter to managing editor and then editor of *American Banker*.

Even though our common professional interests changed, we continued to see each other regularly for lunch and remained friends. When *American Banker* was restructured in the late 1980s, Bill lost his job. Bill described his dismissal as losing an old friend after a 26-year relationship that began when he graduated from college and went to work as a copy editor.

As part of his severance package, he was assigned to an outplacement firm. Outplacement forced him to focus on different career options. It was the first time that Bill ever took a strategic look at his career. In addition to taking aptitude tests, his outplacement counselor worked in the dual capacity as coach and devil's advocate as Bill wavered between finding another job in business journalism or devoting his full attention to Guarionex Press, Ltd., a publishing company he owns and that had already published several books.

Bill was a novice when it came to job hunting. After working for one company his entire career, he didn't have a resumé, nor did he know the rituals of job networking. He was already writing his fifth book and he was running a small press, but Bill decided to return to daily journalism.

After several months as a business editor with the Sunday edition of the *New York Times*, he decided that there was more opportunity with *Newsday* in a similar editorial capacity. Bill continues to operate Guarionex Press as an escape valve and a possible vehicle for retirement.

Downsized on Wall Street

Nancy Wickstrom (early thirties) knows what it's like to lose a high-paying job as a financial manager. Rather than find another administrative position in investment banking, Nancy's solution was more radical.

On the advice of her outplacement counselor, she decided to enter a crafts field. Nancy took a course in wallpapering, combining two of her hobbies, interior design and art, into a new career as an entrepreneur and wallpaperer. (See her profile in Chapter 15.)

His Company Was Acquired

Richard Kavesh's (late thirties) job became redundant when his employer was acquired by another company. When Dick graduated from Hamilton College, he intended to be a college professor like his father. Dick enrolled in a political science doctoral program at the Massachusetts Institute of Technology and within six months decided that academia wasn't for him.

Instead he went to Germany to study German, mostly so he could better understand the classical German composers. After returning to the United States, Dick got a sales job with a small medical instrumentation company. Within two years he was promoted to director of international sales.

"For 11 years, I had a great job with regular overseas trips. It was a wonderful way to enjoy Europes's culture at the company's expense." Matrix Corporation grew from $4 to $100 million in sales, and when it was acquired by a German instrumentation company, Dick's international job was eliminated.

By then, he was making about $100,000. "I was transferred back to domestic sales and treated like a junior salesman. I was being asked to prove myself and at a reduced salary." Perhaps it was Matrix's way to force Dick's hand.

"It was time to do something else. I was too old to be a major league baseball player or start a classical musical career." Dick's career alternative, radio news broadcasting, represented a 180-degree departure from medical instrumentation sales. Because he was single, he was able to consider a career with less income potential than business.

After earning a master's degree in journalism, it took Dick five months to find an entry-level job, where he works the 7 p.m. to 3 a.m. shift as night news editor of a suburban New York radio station.

No Longer in Advertising Sales

Mary McCormick (late forties) came full circle after she lost her job as director of advertising for *McCall's Needleworks & Crafts*

Magazine. It was never stated as such, but Mary learned that the chances of finding another top job in magazine sales were relatively slim. Employers implied that they could just as easily hire younger candidates for less money.

After evaluating different career alternatives, Mary used her college degree in sociology as an entry-level credential to get a job as a caseworker for a social agency. (Her profile appears in Chapter 13.)

THE NEWS COMES IN THE FORM OF EARLY RETIREMENT

Strip away the corporate rhetoric, the hand-holding of human resource experts, and the package of corporate benefits: early retirement often comes at a time of life when executives can least afford it financially and emotionally. To many, it is just another form of saying, "You're fired."

Early retirement has caught all too many executives in their early to midfifties off guard. They expected to retire in their late fifties to early sixties. When they are given early retirement and look for a new job, more often than not they find that their job skills are outdated or prospective employers consider them overpaid.

The alternatives seem clear: retire and live on a reduced income, get another job, which is usually for less pay and often with less responsibility than the previous job, or break stride and start a new career.

Early Retirement from an Insurance Company

Richard Marx's (late fifties) entire academic and business life centered on numbers. After majoring in math at college, he went to work for Mutual Life Insurance of New York as an actuary and eventually became an assistant vice president. When MONY offered him an early retirement package, he computed its financial merits and accepted the offer. He also knew, however, that he needed a second income.

Dick is fortunate. His skill in mathematics is highly portable and can be readily applied to other work in different fields. It eased his transition into a new career as a classroom teacher. Using some of the money from his buyout, he received a master's degree in education, was certified as a teacher in New York State, and now teaches high school math. (His profile appears in Chapter 9.)

From Industry to College Administration

Richard Golden (early sixties) spent nearly 30 years as research and development manager for several major chemical companies. When Arco Chemical Company offered him early retirement, Dick, then 56 and the company's research vice president, accepted.

Two years later, after working as an outplacement counselor advising other deposed corporate executives, Dick, who has a doctorate in chemical engineering, was hired by the Princeton University School of Engineering as an associate dean in charge of administrative functions. (His profile appears in Chapter 9.)

WHEN YOUR CAREER IS STONEWALLED

There comes a time in many careers when the light turns amber, signaling caution. The natural tendency the first time you see this signal is to avoid the warning. When it blinks a second time, then it's time to think of career alternatives. Stonewalling comes in different forms: small or infrequent pay raises from an otherwise financially sound employer, being passed over for promotion or partnership, or an intransigent superior who refuses to relax the rules.

Rather than allow a career to plateau, the alternatives are to resign and take a new position with another organization or start a new career. This is not as difficult as being fired, but the reality of being stonewalled is always the same.

Steven Naru (midthirties) is not the typical career changer, but the inflexibility of military protocol created a convert. After graduating from United States Military Academy (West Point) he was assigned for nearly five years as a missile officer in Germany and was then transferred for another four years as a public relations officer at West Point.

After completing this assignment, his request for a one-year extension at the academy was denied because it was inconsistent with official policy. His career was stonewalled. The Army lost an officer, and Steven, now skilled in media relations, found a higher paying civilian job with a public relations firm. (His profile appears in Chapter 17.).

---◆---

Points to Remember

► "You're fired" are devastating words.
► It's taking longer to get a job these days.
► Outplacement services can help.
► There is more interest in self-employment.
► Prepare a contingency plan in the event you're fired.
► Early retirement and stonewalling often equate with being fired.
► Learn how to fight back.

---◆---

CHAPTER 3

How Do I Know When I'm Ready?

To some it is always tomorrow or after the next rise in the highway. They'd like to work at something else, yet never do.

Some people change careers voluntarily, following a scripted schedule. Others don't have the luxury of delay: change was forced on them without warning. Their jobs were abolished, they were fired, or they were offered a take it or leave it early retirement package.

They must respond immediately. Should they find a new job in the same field using existing skills, or should they do something different? "If you've got 70 years ahead of you, why sit in a company, get your 10 percent raise each year, get promoted, then retire?" is the way that John Hoff, a 26-year-old Californian, explained as the reason for starting his own business. "That just isn't enough of a challenge to me. You haven't smelled the roses along the way."[1]

OVERCOMING INERTIA

If you've ever worked in a large city or in a suburban industrial office park, you're most likely familiar with the lunchtime scene: executives gather in front of the building or eat together in the company's dining room. Their routine rarely varies. They look desperate, like characters in an Edward Hopper painting.

If these executives won the lottery jackpot and achieved what New York State promotes as "a dollar and a dream," you wonder, how might their lives have differed? Most likely very little: they are unfortunately shackled to their jobs. Surely factors other than mortgage, college tuition, and installment payments must be checkmating their lives, or is it fear of striking out in a new direction? This topic is of considerable concern to management consultant and author Robert Waterman.

Writing in *The Renewal Factor*, Waterman points out that change breeds opportunity. "Most of us fear change. Even when our minds say change is normal, our stomachs quiver at the prospect. But for leaders and managers today there is no choice but to change."

Most of the people I interviewed described their career change rather routinely. "I wanted to do my thing." "I just wanted to be my own boss." "I always wanted to teach." They see little cause for excitement that they opened a bookstore in preference to practicing law or they took a teenage hobby and made it the basis of a new career.

Outsiders, however, perceive career changers as romantics. They admire those who have broken with the status quo by training for a new field, used severance pay or early retirement income to buy a business, or relocated so they could combine work and play in a new lifestyle.

ACTING UPON A DREAM

Grove Ely (late fifties) has taken Waterman's renewal factor and applied it to redirecting his own career. A one-time consumer packaging executive turned boat yard and marina operator, Ely links his own changeover with a homemade "grow or die" philosophy.

"When you get up every morning, you have to plan your life in a way that lets you grow. Don't go thinking 'I'm going to hold to what I have.' Because what you hold onto gradually diminishes. If you don't seek new horizons, you disappear." (His profile appears in Chapter 14.)

The Gourmet Cook Challenged to Change Careers

For Ceri Hadda (midthirties), the motivation to change careers was ignited by a different set of circumstances. A gourmet cook and cookbook author, Ceri was challenged to change careers by an offhand remark made at a friend's party. A fellow cook jokingly asked Ceri if she planned to be baking key lime pies for another 10 years.

This rather innocent remark triggered Ceri to rephrase her friend's question. Would she always be making her living as a cook? Should she seek a more demanding challenge? It prodded her to consider alternatives, including medical school.

This was hardly a rash choice: both her father and grandfather were physicians. It was the first time since Ceri graduated from Smith College 12 years earlier that she thought about being a doctor. "In college, I didn't think I was mature enough for medicine. My father has a laissez-faire attitude toward my career. He neither encouraged nor discouraged me."

To qualify for medical school, she enrolled as an evening student in the Hunter College premed program and worked during the day running her catering business and writing food books. In August 1992, Ceri entered the Mt. Sinai School of Medicine, where her goal is to combine her experience in food and nutrition into a career in geriatric medicine.

TAKE A GOOD LOOK IN THE MIRROR

The mechanism that sets off a career change may actually date to our youths. I'm sure that psychologists and behavioral scientists have logical, clinical explanations, but some career changers seem to take a "this is what I always wanted to do and now I'm going to do it" approach, as evidenced by Ray Handley's (mid-forties) career turnaround.

When Handley announced that he would be giving up his estimated $100,000 job as an assistant coach of the New York Giants to enter law school in 1991, he was at the point in his life when he felt a need to do something different.

Handley considered law school in the 1960s when he was a Stanford University student and an All-American back, but he moved with the tides into football coaching. His interest in law was rekindled by law professors he met while he was an assistant coach at Stanford in the early 1980s.

By the time he was hired by the Giants, his coaching status had evolved into being "only a bridesmaid and never the bride." He decided to leave football. Accepted to law school, he deferred admission so he could help the Giants prepare for the 1990 season.

The Giants won the 1991 Super Bowl, and Handley resigned so he could enter law school the following fall. Football fans know the rest of the story. Like a Hollywood film script, his boss, coach Bill Parcell, resigned, and Handley, who was ready to go to law school, was named Parcell's successor.[2]

Once an Actor, Always an Actor

As an Oberlin College student, Paul Nadler (midthirties) wanted to write and teach classical dramatic literature but he delayed acting on his dream. Instead, Paul's mastery in college of computer software qualified him for a well-paid job as a programmer.

In 1988, Paul's favorite uncle gave him some deathbed advice: "Do what you love." Uncle Melvin sowed the seeds by forcing Paul's hand. Reponding to his uncle's challenge, Paul completed a master's degree in theater arts while working as a computer programmer.

When Citibank, N.A., reduced its computer staff and he lost his job, Paul, now married to a *Wall Street Journal* reporter, enrolled in a doctoral program in theater history and took the next academic step in living his Oberlin dream.

She Auditions for a New Career

Sasha von Scherler (midfifties) came to the point in her long theatrical career when she knew it was time for a change. Sasha made her New York debut when she was 19, and over the next 35 years her theatrical credits ranged from Shakespeare to TV commercials.

In the late 1980s, while trying out for a small role, she was asked to return for another audition. Considering her years of theatrical experience, she was infuriated and demeaned by any need for an additional reading, all for a one-minute part.

In an instant, Sasha decided it was time to do something different. Getting the part became incidental. She had no intention of being humiliated professionally again.

Later that day, as she was returning home, she asked the taxi driver to stop just long enough so she could pick up an application for the Hunter College School of Social Work.

She decided to take a similar career route as her husband's, Paul Mayer, who had recently become a psychotherapist after 30 years as a TV scriptwriter. Now that she has a master's degree, Sasha is a full-time staff therapist at an AIDS treatment center.

WHAT HAPPENS WHEN YOU'RE BORED?

We all fear boredom. At an early age, we become adept at avoiding this problem by channeling our energies into other activities. Dr. Judith Meyerowitz (see Chaper 1) says we escape boredom by daydreaming.

Boredom hardly means professional or managerial incompetence; rather it is a signal that perhaps it's time for change.

Alone in Her Studio

Molly Cowgill (early forties), like many creative people, worked alone as an artist. Isolation, as many artists know, often leads to boredom, a problem Molly faced and solved by becoming a doctor.

Following graduation from college, Molly perfected her ceramic skills by attending the New York State College of Ceramics, and then moved to Richmond, Virginia. She set up a studio in her home and gained national recognition for her etched porcelain. Some of her pieces sold for as much as $800 and have been exhibited in the Smithsonian Institution and other museums.

Despite her creative success, Molly was bored, "and with my long hours alone in the studio, I missed interacting with people. I worked as an aide in a nursing home and found it really satisfying. The patients were so appreciative of every bit of attention. With all the problems in the world, it seemed like I could be doing more than making these beautiful little objects."

While helping her sister, a paramedic, to attend medical school, Molly thought about becoming a doctor herself. Following training at the Medical College of Virginia, Molly is a resident in obstetrics and gynecology in Richmond.[3]

THE ENTREPRENEURIAL URGE

All career changers are risk takers. Anyone leaving a safe job for a professional or entrepreneurial career is a risk taker, as the profiles in this book attest. The trend is accelerating as more and more corporate exiles accept the risk of self-employment in preference to the uncertainties of corporate employment. In a 10-year period from 1980 to 1990, the number of sole proprietorships rose from 10 million to nearly 15 million.

Sells One Company and Starts Another

"Tom Wilson" (not his real name) embodies the spirit of the career switcher and entrepreneur. Change is consistent with his lifestyle "I can't believe that at age 22 we are expected to work in the same or similar environment for the next 45 years. We should consider changing careers every 10 years."

Trained as a medical engineer, Tom (midfifties) founded a high-tech electronics company when he was 30 and sold his interest a few years later when the firm had built product and market leadership and had gone public. With some of the proceeds from the stock offering, he started a mail-order company.

With little knowledge of the mail-order business, he applied the business skills learned in previous jobs. Within several years Tom's new company had become a niche specialist in an expanding marketplace. Even with another business success, Tom, the entrepreneur, doubts that this is his last new venture.

Never Liked Being an Employee

Jeffrey Keelan (late thirties) bypassed his previous academic training and work experience in search of a second career. After several years as a department buyer and apparel salesman, Jeff decided it was time to launch his own business even though he had little cash and even less financial borrowing power.

Jeff gambled. He was hardly a skilled craftsman, but he liked being a do-it-yourself worker around his home. After investigating a number of different home crafts, he was attracted to wallpapering because it requires only a small capital investment.

He learned the fundamentals of wallpapering as an apprentice and in the process found that there was a shortage of trained wallpapers. In the late 1980s, Jeff, the entrepreneur, launched the Paperhanging Institute, the only licensed trade school to train wallpapers in the metropolitan New York market. (See his profile in Chapter 15.)

Blindman's Bluff

When we were youngsters, our parents told us first to taste the food before seasoning it with salt. It was an early lesson in decision making. In school we are taught to use research to help reach decisions. At other times, we cease being logical and adopt different agendas. We "throw caution to the wind."

Barry Rein (early fifties) gambled and invested in a business in which he was a complete novice, an approach that was inconsistent with his training as a research chemist and corporate executive. When Barry executed his golden parachute contract, he opted to convert a Victorian home into a bed-and-breakfast inn.

With virtually no experience in home remodeling, he supervised the conversion of a dilapidated three-story, 20-room house into a B&B that could accommodate up to 30 guests. His brochure promised a gourmet breakfast, and Barry had never cooked for that many people. A few days before the first guests arrived, he started to read cookbooks and practice recipes (See his profile in Chapter 14.)

"WHEN THE CAUSE IT IS JUST..."

Whether the goal is law, owning a bookstore, becoming a social worker or a journalist, or teaching high school English, some career changers prefer to work in fields in which their individual efforts might influence social change. When Lee Newcomer was asked why he left private medical practice, took a steep pay cut and went to work for a health care organization, he said, "I'm trying to change medical policy. That's something I couldn't do as a practitioner."[4]

My talks with many career changers indicate that the challenge to help others was perhaps the most important factor motivating them to switch careers.

From Urban Planning to the Clergy

Lynne Grifo's (midthirties) career switch was triggered by her work as a volunteer community activist.

With a master's degree in city planning from Pratt Institute in New York, Lynne spent seven years as an urban planner with several quasi-public development organizations. In her free time, she volunteered to teach homeless children how to read and she served as a lay leader with her local parish church.

"In urban planning, one does not see results very quickly due to long time lags on large projects." On one job, she was responsible for developing the plans for a $600 million urban development project that has yet to be built.

As an alternative, Lynne looked for work in which she could blend an interest in the church and community and public affairs and also find greater job satisfaction. "I wanted to be part of the solution, where I can combine my interest in the church, urban affairs, and social activities in a single career."

Instead of buying a cooperative apartment, Lynne used the money to pay part of her seminary tuition. While a seminarian, she ran a tutoring program for residents of a welfare residence. Ordained an Episcopal priest in 1990, she is now an associate rector in a metropolitan Philadelphia parish, the first step toward meeting her career objectives.

The Cop Turns Minister

Robert Fordham (midfifties) was a Washington, D.C. police officer for almost 25 years. While waiting to take the captain's examination, he found his answer in the ministry. Fordham is one of a number of Washington area black professionals who has gone, as the *Washington Post* headlined, "from the rat race to the saving grace."

What prompted their career changes? They were dissatisfied by the single-mindedness of corporate work and by their inability to find time outside work for social activism.[5]

Finds Teaching More Rewarding Than Merchandising

A childhood experience accelerated Joan Chanwick's (midthirties) entry into education. Joan felt like a square peg in a round hole after eight years as a retail merchandiser and operations manager for the Girl Scouts, Bloomingdale's, and Conran's, Inc.

Even with a series of progressively better retailing jobs, Joan never felt like she had a profession. She enjoyed some aspects of the fast-moving retail business, but she became disinterested in the overly competitive environment.

Her primary interest focused on children. The origins of her interest actually began early in life, when she taught her younger sister, who has cerebral palsy, how to walk. It was this motivation that led Joan to a career change, to train at Teacher's College as an early childhood development teacher.

REFLECTIONS IN THE GLASS CEILING

A lack of significant promotions, window-dressing jobs, and inequitable pay scales contribute to women's decisions to change careers. The women's movement has helped to produce better employment opportunities and, with them, more pronounced career paths in business and the professions. When women find their careers blocked, they move on.

Because of the high personal price that women pay for their careers, many do not settle as readily as men for dead-end jobs, says a Wick & Company study. "The trade-offs and sacrifices usually become most apparent when they are in their early to mid-thirties. That is the time women are most likely to evaluate their current job and, if it falls short of their career expectations, they leave."

Wanted to Be "Top Banana"

"Janet Jones" (not her real name), late thirties, patterns her career change after the Wick study. She recognized her problem even when others believed she was a corporate high achiever: 15 years after she joined the department store chain, Janet, who has a MBA, was earning over $80,000.

Even when the chain downsized, she was told that her job was secure. The company's confidence didn't matter, since Janet had already become bored with retailing. She was also concerned that few women within the company were being promoted to higher supervisory positions. She realized that her career had peaked.

"If you can't make 'top banana,' move on," is how Janet summarized her decision to quit retailing to take a job directing a non-profit community action group.

This Supermommy Takes Action

A generation ago, supermommy had a different persona. If she worked full-time, it was near home in what was then described as a "pink-collar" job as a nurse, teacher, or secretary. In a dramatic shift in scenarios, she now commutes to work, has corporate ambitions, and has the academic and professional credentials to expect recognition.

It's here that a different breed of women has emerged. They are expected by their employers to be supermommies, juggling family and home while working and achieving in a competitive business environment.

As an alternative to the supermommy lifestyle, women are leaving the corporate world with increasing frequency to become entrepreneurs or to train for a different profession in once male-dominated fields, such as law, medicine, and the clergy. The U.S. Labor Department found that more women are becoming sole proprietors or are self-employed. In 1990, 3.1 million women comprised nearly 36 percent of all self-employed workers, a rise of 6 percent in 10 years, when there were 2.1 million self-employed women.

Freed from Being a Supermommy

Susan Lawley (late thirties) has experienced corporate and financial success. In 17 years, she progressed from an entry-level job at AT&T to Bankers Trust Company, where over a 7-year period she was promoted to vice president and earning $225,000 in the bank's investment banking department.

She was recruited by Goldman Sachs & Company as a vice president at an even larger salary, $250,000. Susan was also a supermommy: the wife of Robert, a telecommunciations expert she met at Bankers Trust, and the mother of Greg, then 10. The Lawleys had a combined family income exceeding half a million dollars.

Stress takes its toll. Susan's moment of decision to do something different was triggered when she was driving home from work at 10 p.m. She realized that life is too short for this type of personal sacrifice. Susan left the Wall Street fast track. Within weeks, she set up a corporate training and outplacement firm, Camelot Consulting Group, Inc. and decreased her commute to less than 10 minutes.

Susan's career change did not stop there. When she worked in New York City, she and Robert drove to work together. With their hectic schedules, commuting provided an opportunity to talk. Career switching, however, was never one of the topics on the agenda even though both had reservations about the direction of their careers. A few weeks after Susan left Goldman Sachs, Bob left Bankers Trust to start Gain Communications Inc.

In their new professional life, the Lawleys, who share office space, are pleased with the growth in their consulting practices even though it means a reduced income. Other changes in lifestyle have taken place. They traded in their Jaguar for two U.S.-manufactured cars.

"No longer do we need status symbols. Camelot gives me a higher degree of flexibility than the corporate world. No longer must I accept every assignment. But Camelot is not the end of the line, either. I might do something different in another 5 to 10 years."

------------◆------------

Points to Remember

- ► Act on a dream.
- ► Be willing to break with the past.
- ► Sometimes you're just bored.
- ► Be willing to take risks.
- ► You never liked being an employee.
- ► You want to help others.
- ► Women have special concerns.

------------◆------------

CHAPTER 4

Planning a Career Change

I'm the Otterbourg family career counselor. Ever since their college days nearly a dozen years ago, I've been advising my daughter and son to plan ahead and, above all, think strategically about their careers.

As I was interviewing outplacement consultants for this book, I found that the techniques I suggested to my children are in many ways similar to those consultants use with their clients.

These consultants told me that many of their clients had never prepared a strategic career plan. More often than not, professionals and managers work from job to job and promotion to promotion without ever asking where they are going and how they will get there.

The shock comes when they are suddenly discharged or presented with a take it or leave it retirement package. What are the career alternatives? Find another job in the same field, return to school for additional education, or change careers?

CAREER ASSESSMENT

Not all career changers are motivated toward a specific career. After years of working in the marketplace or as a lawyer, a number of people are unsure of the next step. Other than their present skills, they have little knowledge of other aptitudes. Yet before making a career change, you need to know more about yourself. For some, aptitude tests and career counseling furnish clues and, perhaps, an introduction to a new career.

"Look at your personal history" is how career counselor Nella Barkley, president of Crystal-Barkley Corporation, advises her clients. Like many career consultants, she emphasizes the importance of learning and building a career around assets, not liabilities. Nella's firm advises clients to prepare a biography. This is an approach that you can easily handle on your own.

"Analyze both work and non-work experiences—everything from editing a high school yearbook to how you earned your most recent promotion. In each case, think about the skills you used to accomplish what you did. Then write each skill on an index card, one per card. Keep looking over your life and writing down skills until the stack piles up...a stack of 300 to 1000 cards is not unusual. Doing this exercise helps redefine who you are and what you want from your career."

How Did Jeff Fox Find His Career?

A pile of index cards may help to produce a career road map, but it was one technique that was at first alien to Jeffrey Fox (early forties) and his approach to career planning.

After Jeff resigned as president of Fox & Geller, Inc., the software firm he founded, he knew only that he wanted to strike out in a new direction. Computers would not be the basis of the new career. Otherwise, he had little idea of the direction in which he would move.

Before he was ready to really make any commitment, he enrolled in a midlife career-counseling course, read career guidance books, and spent nearly six months studying different career options.

If Jeff had used Nella Barkley's system, one of the cards would have signaled a lifelong interest in journalism. Jeff entered journalism school 10 months after he left Fox & Geller, the opening step in his second career as a magazine journalist. (See his profile in Chapter 17.)

Testing Confirms a New Career

After 15 years as a St. Petersburg, Florida realtor, Bob Grytten (early fifties) decided to look at other careers. Bob was unhappy with changes in the tax laws and how they might affect the real estate portfolios he managed.

Looking to change careers, he was undecided on his direction. Johnson O'Connor aptitude tests started the process; they helped him learn more about himself. They showed that he had strong aptitudes to work in a science and technology-related job.*

---

*The Myers-Briggs Type Indicator and the Strong Vocational Interest Inventory are two other recognized aptitude tests used in career planning.

After evaluating the results, he was further convinced of the need to change careers. He considered a number of different careers, and he selected nature photography based on an earlier interest in photography as a hobby and its correlation with science and technology. Bob learned his new trade on the job, where he works as a freelance commercial photographer, travel writer and editor of a travel photography newsletter.

GATHERING THE FACTS

Columnist Ann Landers warns divorced individuals about the dangers of remarrying the same type of person. Career changing follows a similar path: to leave one career for another does not necessarily solve life's problems. The secret is to minimize risk, a point that outplacement firms stress to their clients. As part of the outplacement cycle (much of which you can accomplish on your own without professional guidance), clients are encouraged to read career books, attend how-to career guidance workshops, take aptitude test, and evaluate different career alternatives.

Even with career counseling and aptitude tests, what do you really know about commercial photography, retailing, or cooking? Will your decision be based on facts and experience rather than illusion? Whether the goal is the ministry or journalism, there's no substitute for "touching the merchandise."

Volunteer or work part-time as an apprentice before making a new career commitment. Medical schools go one step further. To qualify for admission, they encourage and in some instances even specifiy that applicants work part-time or serve as a volunteer in a hospital or clinic. Theology seminaries give potential career changers psychological tests to weed out the romantics.

ATTEND CAREER WORKSHOPS

We live in a career changers' paradise. Trade and professional associations conduct workshops to encourage newcomers to consider their fields. The American Booksellers Association conducts an annual workshop for prospective owners of bookstores. Nearly every college and university sponsors at least one annual career workshop. Others are more ambitious and conduct elaborate extension programs.

The New York University Center for Career and Life Planning has fashioned a special curriculum for career changers. It offers a menu of general seminars on midcareer assessment, as well as specific seminars on career changing for lawyers, second careers in teaching, and alternative careers for nurses.

When Michael Levine (midthirties) decided to leave publishing for public relations, he learned the rudiments of his new career at a series of adult education courses at the University of California–Los Angeles. This provided the incentive to quit publishing and start what has become one of the nation's larger publicity firms in the entertainment field.

Unsure of the commitment a nursing career entailed, Marilyn Owens (late thirties) attended several different nursing school workshops before she decided to leave her job as an executive secretary and become a nurse. (See her profile in Chapter 10.)

EXPLORING THE MARKET

The army calls them "sappers," the soldiers who precede the tanks and infanty and, with their special electronic equipment, detect land mines. Career changers have similar opportunities to sample the menu before eating the meal.

Don't underestimate the power of market research. Get the facts. Take a do-it-yourself approach. Make field trips. Visit other businesses. Talk to competitors.

Visiting B&B Inns

Penni Johnson (midforties) and Susan Moehl (midthirties) decided to explore the bed-and-breakfast market before making a commitment. Their objective was to open an inn. What they lacked were facts.

Susan, a corporate marketer, and Penni, a lawyer, spent their vacations visiting inns in different parts of the country, talking to inn owners and gaining practical know-how that led to their building an urban inn in Kansas City, Missouri. (See their profile in Chapter 14.)

The Barnetts, Eve (early forties), a nurse, and Norman (midfifties), an investment banker, decided it was time to leave New England for a more rural lifestyle and the opportunity to own a farm. They selected the Pacific Northwest. As part of their investigation, they made seven trips to Oregon in one year before buying Youngberg Farm, where they grow Pinot noir grapes, raise sheep, and run a small inn. (See their profile in Chapter 16.)

FURTHERING YOUR EDUCATION

The College Board, a monitor of trends in higher education, reports that 6 million people in the United States aged 25 and older are enrolled in a college course or program and more than one-half of the 1.7 million graduate students are over 30 years of age.

Adults rarely learn for the sheer pleasure of learning; the interest is pragmatic. They learn because they want to use the knowledge at work or at home, says Carol Aslanian, who directs the College Board Office of Adult Learning Services. It is hardly a surprise that approximately 70 percent of the courses taken by adults are in career-related fields, such as business, computers or information science, education, and health care.

Adults also learn so they may cope more effectively with change in their lives. They are making a transition from one status in life to another. This factor motivates adults to learn, and they learn what they need to know to be successful in their new work.[1]

Would-be career changers have an opportunity to learn new skills at undergraduate- and graduate-level evening and weekend classes and accredited correspondence courses. Courses in most professions and at most levels are conducted for the convenience of working students.

Except medicine, nearly all other professions and skills can be learned while a career changer continues to work. For over 75 years, the Columbia University Graduate School of Journalism offered only a daytime course of study. In 1991 it introduced an evening and weekend program to attract students othewise excluded from daytime study.

A word of advice when taking professional development courses: discretion is in order when studies conflict with an employer's corporate mission. Even with scheduling courses at night and on weekends, a possible conflict of interest exists for potential career changers.

When you're working for a bank and you tell your boss that you intend to get a MBA or law degree, chances are your employer will reimburse part or nearly all of the tuition. When you're working for the same bank and your objective is medical school, however, how do you ask for reimbursement to study anatomy, chemistry, and zoology? Taking non–business-related courses and asking for reimbursement may place your job in jeopardy.

Correspondence schools represent another way to learn or enhance skills in anticipation of a career change. This can also be done in the privacy of the home without tipping off employers about an impending career switch.

Be aware of correspondence schools. Before enrolling in any course, make sure the program is currently certified by the department of education in your state. This is a practical way to ensure the legitimacy of the school and its curriculum.

Correspondence schools attract career changers: of the 20,000 correspondent students enrolled at the New York Institute of Photography, 11,000 are over 35 years of age, and 6500 of the 15,000 home-study students at the Sheffield School of Interior Design are in this same age group.

The Single Mother Goes to Law School

Nobody ever said it is easy to hold a full-time job and go to evening school. Susan Rolon (midthirties), a single mother with a nine-year-old son and a teenage daughter, works Monday through Friday, six hours a day, as a New York City elementary school teacher.

Her four-year law school routine is tightly orchestrated: she gets up at 6 a.m. and walks her children to school, and when her school workday ends Susan travels eight miles by subway to Fordham University Law School, attends classes for several hours, uses the library, returns home to eat and study, and goes to bed after 1 a.m. (See her profile in Chapter 11.)

Studying for the Ministry at Night

Most clergy take theology training as full-time day students. Hugh Hildesley (early fifties), rector of an Episcopal church, is an exception. A senior officer and auctioneer for Sotheby's, Hugh attended a theology extension program conducted by the Episcopal Diocese of New York. For four years, he averaged five hours of sleep a night and gave up all social life, and since he was traveling extensively on business, he studied on airplanes and in hotel rooms. (See his profile in Chapter 12.)

Studing Law at Evening School Was His Only Way

Night school meant something else to James Ruane (late fifties). It was the only way he could get both an undergraduate and law school education. By day, most of the residents of 805 Park Avenue in New York knew Ruane only as one of the building's doormen, but across the Hudson River in Newark, New Jersey he was a member of the Seton Hall University Law School class of 1991.

For four years as a law school student, James rose at 4:30 a.m., commuted by subway from Brooklyn to New York and worked until 4 p.m., then took a 20-mile train trip to Seton Hall, returning home after classes by 11:15 for two more hours of study. Although younger lawyers were finding it difficult to find entry-level jobs, Ruane, as a result of meeting a lawyer in a coffee shop, was employed at a New York labor and personal injury law firm.[2]

THE NEED TO CUT COSTS

Set aside the financial spread sheets. If you're analyzing the financial returns, then career changing can be a risky investment. Other than medicine, the law, and some businesses, chances are slim that former corporate salaries will be duplicated.

Financial planning for career changers is much the same as planning for any major individual or family event—buying a home, a college education, or retirement. It means allocating sufficient funds in advance to cover education during a period when you're out of the job market or during the start-up period when establishing a new business. Above all, it means knowing the economics of whatever profession or business you're planning to enter.

Career changing and a nest egg go hand in hand.

Many of the career switchers in *It's Never Too Late* live on reduced incomes, using savings that were accumulated specifically to make the career change financially possible, or are subsidized by a working spouse's full-time salary. Some relocate to areas where living expenses are lower. Nearly all career changers take a financial risk by leaving othewise secure corporate and professional jobs. Then again, as already noted, career changers are risk takers.

Only a few career changers I interviewed are as financially fortunate as Jack Berdy (midforties), who sold his $100 million publicly owned software company during his second year in medical school, or social activist Marvin Lender, who was one of the owners of a family owned bagel company that was acquired for $65 million. Nearly all others became career changers by first accumulating savings and then using the income to support the transition to a new career. Simply put, career changers, regardless of field, need to have an entrepreneurial attitude.

When Geoffrey Quinn (midthirties) was accepted to Cornell Medical College, he turned down the opportunity as a California resident to attend one of that state's cost-free medical schools. He and his wife, Chris, rented their condominium apartment in New York, moved to affordable student housing, reduced out-of-pocket expenses to a minimum, and used some of their savings to minimize medical school debt. Other than a maternity leave, Chris continued to work as a TV news writer for CBS. (See Geoffrey's profile in Chapter 10.)

The Reverend William Stokes (midthirties) and his wife, Susan, were literally money magicians during Bill's three years as a seminarian. They had no other choice since the Stokes are the parents of four children and the guardians of a live-in nephew.

A year before he entered the seminary, they went on an austerity program, and William and Susan worked several jobs to accumulate additional savings. While he was a student, Bill worked in the seminary's dining room and Susan worked full-time for three years as a hotel administrator. It was their way to minimize debt. (See his profile in Chapter 12.)

Some career changers find it difficult to meet expenses in their new work. By necessity, they straddle two worlds during their transition. Elaine Knechtel (midthirties), previously a $55,000 a year publicist for high-tech companies, trained to be a gourmet cook. She now runs a catering service and gives cooking lessons.

While her cooking business is growing, her income is limited. Until she is self-sufficient as a cook, Elaine balances her books by working as a part-time account executive in a small West Coast public relations firm. (See her profile in Chapter 14.)

Jane Brook Barba (midforties), previously a designer of children's clothes, studied horticulture and then established American Cottage Gardens, which designs small gardens for townhouses, terraces, and corporate offices. To meet expenses, Jane works as a part-time member of the New York Botanical Gardens professional staff. (See her profile in Chapter 16.)

The first two years after Murray Hulse (midfifties) became a custom furniture maker, he operated his craft business from his cellar woodworking shop. Although limited in space, it enabled Murray to control overhead costs. When volume grew and he needed more equipment and a full-time assistant, he moved Time & Again Furnishings to a separate location. (See his profile in Chapter 15.)

---◆---

Points to Remember

► Prepare your own strategic plan.

► Take stock of your capabilities.

► Have an open mind.

► Gather facts on new careers.

► Explore possible new markets and careers.

► Career changers are returning to school.

► Watch your expenses.

---◆---

CHAPTER 5

The Art of Piggybacking

A common practice among career switchers is to minimize risk by avoiding 180-degree changes. Even when a new career appears radically different from the previous career, switchers have reduced some of the risk by recycling old skills.

BASE YOUR CAREER CHANGE ON EXPERIENCE

Don't run away from your past. If you're a good writer, this skill transcends most careers. It's not surprising that my dentist repairs antique clocks as a hobby: both require an ability to work with small parts. Most of the career changers profiled in this book have piggybacked many of their skills in their new work.

Support systems exist to show potential career changers how to adapt past skills to new careers. WEORC (an old English word for *work* and pronounced the same way) helps Roman Catholic priests and nuns make the changeover from the clergy to "civilian" life. WEORC recommends that former priests and nuns use their community relations skills to their advantage as social workers and community relations activists.

Herbert Hezel (late fifties) left the Jesuit Order in the mid-1970s after serving as the superintendent for all Jesuit schools in the Philippines. His desire to help people proved to be an important asset in becoming a successful corporate outplacement consultant. (See his profile in Chapter 13.)

The Patrolmen's Benevolent Association of New York City finds that many cops have good people-to-people skills, and it advises members who are about to retire to consider careers in sales, community relations, and personnel.

The Priest Turns Journalist

Donald Casey (midfifties) is a public affairs specialist whose previous career combined the training and skills of a priest, missionary, and journalist. These multiple talents permitted Don to change careers more easily. Starting with junior high school, Don received the balance of his education while training to be a Maryknoll priest. He was ordained at 27. Unlike other religious and secular orders, the Maryknoll Fathers trains priests to serve as administrators, educators, or journalists.

Don's interest was journalism, and he was sent to the Columbia University Graduate School of Journalism for professional training. The next 10 years were spent as a Latin American specialist, traveling and writing on the area.

After leaving the Maryknolls in 1973, Don, who is fluent in Spanish and an expert on Latin American affairs, went to work as a writer for the United Nations Development Corporation. He later used his accumulated communications skills to start a public affairs agency with another former Maryknoll priest.

Vermont's Governor Is a Physician

One expects to find Dr. Howard B. Dean (midforties), an internist, in a medical setting. This career has been on hold since August 14, 1991, when Richard Snelling, then governor of Vermont, died of a heart attack.

Dean, lieutenant governor since 1987 and previously a state legislator for three years, is no newcomer to politics. He majored in political science at Yale University, and before going to medical school, he considered teaching. As a practicing physician, he worked as a volunteer in Jimmy Carter's 1980 presidential campaign and was a delegate to the Democratic national convention.

A medical background has decided advantages in making political decisions since 10 percent of the nation's gross national product is spent on health care. As the only governor with medical training, Dean is applying his knowledge of medicine to his job. He was instrumental in the passage of legislation that will give Vermont residents universal health care by 1995.

He finds that medicine trained him to listen to people, to learn about their concerns, and to ask tough questions and analyze them rationally before deciding on a course of action.[1]

Uses Medical Skills as a Lawyer

John Gilman (late forties) is also a physician, but he gave up medicine in the mid-1980s to become a lawyer. Like Governor Dean, he also majored in political science at college. Instead of law school, Gilman completed medical training in 1974 and then ran a solo ophthalmology practice in Santa Rosa, California.

"I always wanted to be a lawyer and I knew someday that I would get my law degree. Ten years of medical practice seemed like enough. I missed San Francisco and wanted to do something else with my life. I had saved enough money to take care of my needs for five years. After selling my practice, I initially considered buying another one in San Francisco but ruled it out so I could get on with my dream of being a lawyer." After traveling for one year and another year changing professional gears in anticipation of law school, Gilman entered law school.

Unlike some doctors who become lawyers, Gilman has avoided what could have been a highly lucrative career as a malpractice or forensic legal specialist or as a lawyer for a pharmaceutical company. Instead he works at 25 percent of his former medical income for the politically active California Medical Association.

His new career blends his knowledge of medicine, law, and political science. As the only doctor on the association's legal staff, he has a decided professional advantage because he knows how doctors think and he can communicate with them better than most lawyers.

An Electrician Turns Trade School Teacher

Victor Tucker (early sixties) spent 40 years as an electrician and foreman. Victor was only a high school graduate, but this did not prevent him from becoming a high school vocational teacher. Several years ago, when Polaroid Corporation offered him early retirement, he took advantage of his employer's teacher-training program to qualify for a vocational teacher's certificate in Massachusetts. (See his profile in Chapter 9.)

A Common Thread Binds Several Careers

Reading Frank McCoy's (early forties) resumé, one might consider him a job hopper. Frank, now senior editor for *Black Enterprise* magazine, says that a common thread binds a series of jobs and careers into a single package. Just as important, each new career builds on the one before. Throughout his career, he has continually been a political activist, starting as a student at the University of Massachusetts and then at the Tuft University Fletcher School of Law & Diplomacy.

Following Tufts, he worked in a series of jobs: in the Far East as a financial analyst, for a human rights conference in Sri Lanka, and on the Chemical Bank international banking staff handling loan portfolios.

By then, he was interested in journalism. With no credentials in the field, he took a year off to earn a journalism degree. Frank then freelanced for a number of business publications, was a staff writer for *Business Week Magazine*, and left to join *Black Enterprise* as an editor.

McCoy finds that his varied business and political experiences permit him to move with ease from one field to another. "Even when I took a job with Chemical Bank, it was never with the intention of staying forever but rather it was another way to learn how money was used."

The Investment Banker Teaches Banking

After returning from Oxford University in the mid-1960s, where he was a Rhodes Scholar, David Beim (early fifties) began his Wall Street career. He entered investment banking at a time of unprecedented growth in the financial field.

Over the next 25 years, David worked for the First Boston Corporation, Bankers Trust Company, and Dillon Read & Company, Inc. as a key member of their investment banking groups. Throughout this period, he never lost sight of his goal to be a teacher someday. "I always knew I wanted to teach, and when I got married my wife actually expected I would be a college professor rather than an investment banker."

Wall Street started to peak in the late 1980s, the crash of October 1987 signaling the end of investment banking's golden age.

"When I joined Dillon Read as a partner, I also started to teach part-time at Columbia's business school. By this time in my career, I had made a lot of money so the idea of making even more was less of a concern." The opportunity came when he left Dillon Read to become a professor of international banking at Columbia.

BORROWING FROM THE PAST

Changing careers is at times like rummaging in an attic with its stored collection of memorabilia. Attics often produce objects from the past that can be applied in the present, an approach that outplacement consultant Claudia Gentner (late thirties) employed in her own career.

Trained as a librarian with a master's degree in information science, Claudia established and then directed the American

Cyanamid Company business information center. Different from most corporate libraries, which collect primarily research materials, American Cyanamid's library concentrates on providing the staff with strategic corporate and marketing information.

When former Cyanamid marketing executive John Guthery established Seagate Associates Inc. in the early 1980s, he asked Claudia to join the outplacement firm as a principal. Although she had no human resource or career-counseling experience, the usual skills associated with outplacement, she brought a different dimension to the firm.

She applies the business information center concept to Seagate's mission of helping clients select new jobs or careers. Toward this end, Claudia has developed several computerized data bases, a proprietary software system, and other automated tools that prepare Seagate clients for job searches and interviews.

The Rabbi Uses His Legal Skills

After a few years as an associate of a large Boston corporate law firm, Carl Perkins (midthirties) resigned and entered the Jewish Theological Seminary. Until then, Carl, a Haverford College and Harvard University Law School graduate, assumed that he would someday become a partner in this or some other firm.

Influenced by Rabbi Simcha Kling, his late father-in-law and mentor, Carl moved easily from one professional environment to the other. "Compared with the rabbinate, the law is rather narrow. As a rabbi, I can use my interpersonal skills to better advantage. Unlike a lawyer, I'm not forced to be an advocate but rather I have the opportunity to look at both sides of an issue."

Even as a rabbinical student and rabbi in a suburban Boston temple, however, Carl says that his legal training sharpened his analytic skills and improved his problem-solving abilities.

What Do Music and Computer Software Have in Common?

Eric Gaer (early forties) didn't know how to turn on a computer in the early 1980s when he joined a small California software company as director of marketing, but experience in the music business eased Eric's transition into computer marketing. Eric previously spent 10 years in a series of music-related jobs: owner of a music store, editor of a music magazine, promotion manager of an acoustics company, and principal in an advertising agency specializing in music accounts.

"These were whimsical businesses, and since I was now married with several children, I decided to find steadier work." His timing was perfect. Software companies, faced with a shortage of trained personnel, were looking outside the industry for managers with related experience. Eric found that computer marketing and the music business both required lively marketing. Although he knew little about computers, Eric applied his music industry promotional skills to the marketing of computers.

In early 1992, he made another career change. He left his job as marketing director of a $50 million laser printing company and started an interactive multimedia business, where he blends high-tech marketing with his knowledge of radio and television broadcasting, which he had learned in college 20 years before.

A TV Journalist Enters Academia

Joan Konner (late fifties) has been dean of Columbia's Graduate School of Journalism since the late 1980s. Until then, Joan spent nearly 25 years writing and producing public service television documentaries, network television news, and public affairs programs.

When she was named dean, Joan thought at first that there were few similarities between TV and academia. She soon found a number of skills that were indeed transferable: both jobs call for an ability to understand, report, and interpret what's occurring in different cultures, along with an ability to make things happen. In TV, this means producing a news or documentary program and, at Columbia, running a school.

Unlike some career changers, such as David Beim, who first bridged the academic world as adjunct faculty members, Joan made the change abruptly, with no previous academic experience.

Medicine Provides an Entrée to Wall Street

The turn of events in the professional life of Dr. Lindsay Rosenwald are unique. When he was in medical school, he started to question why he was there. It was an interesting question, because Lindsay was a business administration major at Pennsylvania State University.

Even as a medical student, he continued to read the *Wall Street Journal* and actively invest in the market. "I managed a lot of money for doctors and my professors and did some consulting for health care companies."

Lindsay finished medical school and his residency and practiced internal medicine for several years before switching full-time to finance. Medical training was a decided asset in finding a job as a health care industry specialist, first as a financial analyst and then as an investment banker.

In 1991, he founded the Castle Group Ltd., a venture capital and merchant banking firm that provides funding and financial advisory services to small and midsized health care and biotechnology companies. Half of the 26-person staff have medical degrees or doctorates in the life sciences.

Lindsay finds that being a medical doctor offers advantages not available to many of his Wall Street peers: it is easier to network with medical personnel and speak their language, to read medical journals intelligently, and to sift through medical information in search of potential investment opportunities.

Points to Remember

- ► Learn to recycle past skills.
- ► Borrow from the past.
- ► Career changers are salvagers.
- ► Career changing is not a way to escape.
- ► Using past skills helps to minimize the risk.
- ► Recognize the common threads in your past work.

CHAPTER 6

Finding a New Lifestyle

The term "lifestyle" seems to be universally applied to describe nearly every aspect of contemporary life. Even with its current overuse, lifestyle is a relatively new word in our vocabulary. Webster's Ninth New Collegiate Dictionary in fact cites 1946 as the year of its unofficial birth.

Half a century earlier, the economist Thorstein Veblen furnished a nineteenth century spin to lifestyle in *The Theory of the Leisure Class*, when he noted that "conspicuous consumption of valuable goods is a means of reputability to the gentleman of leisure."

In 1926, Henry Ford defined leisure more pragmatically and with a middle-class flavor by closing his factories on Saturdays. Ford rationalized that an increase in leisure time would support an increase in consumer spending, not least on automobile travel and automobiles.[1]

Lifestyle, as we know it today, is actually a post-World War II outgrowth of the leisure concept. It was formulated and injected into our vocabulary by returning GI's seeking to combine job, home, and leisure time in a single package. Lifestyle refers to how and where we work, the types of work we do, the clothes we wear, the foods we eat, and how we play.

Leisure consumes a chunky yet still undetermined part of our work week. The statistics are at best sketchy. One survey conducted in the late 1980s by the National Research Center of the Arts concluded that the U.S. public spends a median of nearly 17 hours of leisure time each week, less than half the time reported by both the University of Maryland and the University of Michigan Survey Research Center.

One's lifestyle is reflected in the social habits of each passing generation. The yuppies of the 1980s were the decade's ultimate lifestyle seekers, yet they were no more shocking in their style of living than the flappers of the 1920s. Both groups were simply trying to create an unique lifestyle for the times. The only thing that seems to change from one generation to the next is how to interpret lifestyle.

Trendsetters like to say that yuppism disappeared with the 1990s. Where has it gone, and what has replaced it? If anything, yuppism has been silenced to a large extent by corporate downsizing and the lagging economy. The signs are everywhere. The two-income family in many instances now has only one wage earner. Overtime work has been reduced. Consumer confidence continues to falter. As workers at all levels feel uncertain about their jobs, the yuppie's image lies dormant.

Until now, there has been no dominant replacement for the yuppie lifestyle even though the new generation of 20 and 30 year olds appears to be focusing on a lifestyle that emphasizes values and quality of life. We can be sure once a replacement for yuppism has established a firm foothold, the trendsetters will rename and retitle it, to which marketing consultant Judith Langer adds, "values don't change overnight. Lifestyles don't change overnight."

If anything, the trendsetters have rediscovered the baby-boomers, a name that was rarely used during the heyday of yuppism. Who are the baby-boomers? They are the generation born between 1945 and 1960, and some of them were yuppies.

Marketers are already at work devising lifestyle scenarios to take the oldest of the baby-boomers, who turn 50 in 1995, into their retirement in the early part of the twenty-first century.

Most interesting of all, the yuppies and baby-boomers represent the largest source of potential career switchers. The baby-boomer generation has already positioned itself as a unique group within the employment market. The Conference Board pointed out in a 1991 study on career planning that "this generation has already demonstrated that individual careers take precedence over company loyalty. In contrast with older workers, younger employees find career switching and job hopping compatible with their life goals."

The baby-boomers are of the age, the education, and the temperament to become a generation of career changers.

HOW CAREER CHANGERS DEFINE LIFESTYLE

Lifestyle means different things to different people. Consumer marketers glibly translate lifestyle in terms of leisure and pleasure outside the workplace. This is symbolized by the single 27-year-old engineer who seeks a lifestyle that permits him or her to design computer chips, work in jeans, and at the end of the business day drive a few miles in a Mazda convertible to windsurf. Professional skills, job performance, and corporate advancement are important factors, but not to the point that they transcend lifestyle.

As we grow older and marry, new interests appear; surfboards are traded for vacation homes, golf, and more sedentary hobbies. In the course of the next 10 to 20 years, we also accumulate baggage, or what the Romans called *impedimenta*—mortgage, time payments, and college tuitions—which alter lifestyle patterns even more.

Although windsurfing was once as critical as work to the 27-year-old engineer, the older engineer discovers new priorities. Job and career become even more important. Is it fun, and is it challenging? Am I continuing to learn and grow professionally? How's the pay? How do I feel about my job at the end of the day? These are questions career changers ask themselves.

Then there are the unknowns—corporate layoffs, downsizing, and early retirement—which translate simply to "you're fired." Now what about lifestyle? Do we continue to define it in materialistic terms, or does lifestyle have a more fundamental meaning?

HOW IMPORTANT IS LOCATION?

As the Joad family in John Steinbeck's *The Grapes of Wrath* realized during their Oklahoma to California migration, a new and perhaps better lifestyle is not always obtainable by relocating. At a recent dinner, I sat next to a woman who told me of two doctor friends, a husband and wife anesthesiology team, who moved to one of the Caribbean islands in search of a more relaxed lifestyle.

"I'm sure they have lots of time to sail and enjoy the tropical lifestyle," I said. "Hardly," was the reply, "There are only two other anesthesiologists on the island, and they're working longer hours than ever before."

When I ran a public relations firm, I learned a lesson in comparative lifestyles. Many of my clients were located in suburban communities and smaller cities up and down the East Coast. When I visited these companies, I envied one particular aspect of what appeared a most pleasant lifestyle: the door-to-door drive for most of the executives was rarely more than 20 minutes.

At that time, I was commuting over two hours a day by bus. I found out, however, that their work week was longer than mine. They got to work earlier and stayed later than I did. I tried to avoid early evening meetings in the name of commuting, but they often held 6 p.m. and Saturday morning meetings. They had an *open-ended workday*, but mine was structured to some extent by my daily commute.

My friend Patrick Monroe (early fifties) took location and made it the focus of his career change. Pat was motivated by two factors: to become self-employed and to work in an area with easy access to recreational facilities.

Pat left metropolitan New York and his job as general manager of a rubber goods company and bought a clothing store in Manchester Center, a small Vermont town that is a regional retail hub and adjacent to a number of ski slopes. Pat works upward of 70 hours a week, longer hours than he did as a corporate executive, but he's able at the last moment to take an afternoon off to go skiing, something that was impossible in his urban jobs. (See his profile in Chapter 14.)

Other would-be career changers are not as fortunate as Pat. They lack his mobility. Family members are anchored to jobs and to their community. Many job seekers soon discover that their skills are not portable. You might want to relocate and change careers, but a wife or husband cannot always be assured of finding a new job.

Location is a critical factor in recruiting personnel and in building new corporate facilities. Companies headquartered in recreational areas "sell the sizzle, not the steak" in their employment ads.

Lifestyle is used regularly as the bait in corporate recruitment advertisement, ranging from "Join the Navy and See the World" to the Desert Hospital ad for staff nurses in the *Journal of Nursing*: "The living is easy in Palm Springs, CA, one of the world's great resort areas. Palm Springs is a mild climate with easy access to fantastic winter sports areas. It is truly a winter wonderland...the best of all possible worlds."

Lifestyle motivated IBM Corporation when it opened an engineering facility in Burlington, Vermont. Although several hundred miles from Boston and New York City, IBM had little trouble attracting qualified engineers and technicians. Skiing, boating, and camping were the lifestyle attractions.

Location as an end in itself can be a smoke screen. Lifestyle is not necessarily defined by ease of access to summertime boating and mountain climbing. Karen Glance (midthirties) knows from experience that location sometimes proves to be deceptive.

Karen left New York City and moved to St. Paul, Minnesota and a new job as a vice president of the Sears Roebuck and Company subsidiary, but her lifestyle hardly changed. She was working a 65-hour work week and had little time to enjoy the tangible benefits of a six-figure salary. Karen discovered that lifestyle is not affected by location but rather by the job.

High-pressure jobs exist regardless of location. She left Sears, bought a retail business, and continues to work long hours. The difference is that she's now the boss. This was Karen's way of controlling her lifestyle. (See her profile in Chapter 14.)

THERE'S MORE TO LIFE THAN MONEY

If you fail to realize the "do what you love and the money will follow" concept, relocating does have its financial advantages. Consumer expenditure studies show that it costs about 16 percent, or $5500, less to live in the rural United States even though higher paying jobs are found in the larger cities. Even among doctors, the highest paid professionals, *Medical Economics Magazine* reports that urban physicians net $142,590, compared with $132,120 in surburban and $117,610 in rural practices.

According to a 1991 survey commissioned by Hilton Hotels Corporation, leisure time, not money, is becoming the status symbol of the 1990s. Finding enough time for both work and personal lives has become so critical that nearly two-thirds of those surveyed say that they would be willing to exchange less pay for more time off.

These findings notwithstanding, John Robinson of the University of Maryland, who conducted the Hilton study, concedes that the high cost of living permits only one-third of those surveyed to actually reduce their work load in the 1990s. All too many people use their leisure time to work another job.

The U.S. public spends its leisure time with families, relaxing, traveling, crafts and hobbies, working around the house and gardening, and attending school. This lifestyle differs for career changers who have traded in established work schedules, paid vacations, and holidays for heavier work loads.

At a time when peers of older career changes are starting to reduce their professional commitments and work pace, the 55-year-old bed-and-breakfast operator or law student puts in the work hours normally associated with a person half their age.

Lifestyle, as career changers point out, means more than relocating, going to work without a necktie, or having more free time. A well-paying corporate job has certain advantages, but when you work for yourself 75 hours a week and you are doing something you want to do, your work *is* your total lifestyle.

LIFESTYLE IS IN FLUX IN THE CORPORATE WORLD

Not everyone can walk away from the high-paying job in search of an improved lifestyle. The ideal scenario is a corporate environment in which lifestyle is emphasized and integrated into the job. Yet studies show that senior executives are not the beneficiaries of corporate lifestyle trends.

If anything, they work exceedingly long hours, a point supported by a study prepared by Korn/Ferry International, an executive search firm, that indicated that U.S. executives work 56 hours a week, 16 hours longer than lower level managers within the same organization, and they average between 12 and 16 vacation days per year, half the number given to Western European employees.

Corporate management is concerned with the lifestyle image. Toward this end, they have implemented job sharing, part-time work, and home-based work, and compressed work weeks to recruit and retain employees. To date, these programs, which are growing in popularity, are designed primarily for low- to midlevel administrative jobs.

Even with the fanfare of publicity that sabbaticals and leaves seem to attract, the Conference Board reports that relatively few corporations have demonstrated interest in sabbaticals and related extended leave programs. If anything, these represent another dimension of work force flexibility, and, says the Conference Board, "they are part of the 'kit of tools' companies must have to compete in the marketplace for the skills they need and want."[2]

There is an irony in flexible scheduling, sabbatical, and leave of absence programs. These methods are intended to increase employee productivity, but they also have the potential to stimulate career changing. Employees working a compressed four-day work week have the opportunity to learn new skills, find a job in another field, or even operate a business. Leaves of absence or sabbaticals provide an opportunity to explore different career options.

How Sculley of Apple Computer Views Sabbaticals

John Sculley is a gambler when it comes to sabbaticals, and he's willing to take the risk, offering them liberally to Apple Computer, Inc. employees. Sculley recognizes the importance of sabbaticals in the lifestyle of its employees. When interviewed by *Fortune Magazine*, he commented on his sabbatical, which he spent in Maine, 3000 miles away from Apple's California headquarters.

"There is a significant difference between vacations and sabbaticals. When people go on vacation, they go for two or three weeks. The first week they collapse and rejuvenate. The last couple of weeks they begin counting the days, saying 'when I get back, I've got to do this.' When you go on sabbatical, you know that you are really going away. You start to think about things very differently....It is one of the best investments a corporation can make in its top executives to keep their minds fresh and get them to broaden the bandwidth of their thinking....Some people go on sabbatical and never come back. That's a risk companies have to take. But I think it's a risk well worth taking."[3]

A Potential Rabbi Returns to His Law Practice

Sculley's concern that sabbaticals breed potential corporate turnover is a gamble that Stephen Axinn's (early fifties) law firm partners accepted when they offered him a six-month paid leave so he could decide whether he wanted to be a rabbi.

"I didn't know who I was, whether I was a lawyer just taking some time off or a fledgling rabbinical intern shedding a life." Six months later, Axinn, who had become a much happier person as a result of his studies, missed the demands of his antitrust litigation job and returned to his legal practice.[4]

THE HOME OFFICE COMES OF AGE

Technology in the form of home office computers and communications equipment is helping to encourage career changing. Telecommuting for many workers is already a reality. Market researchers like Link Resources Corporation estimate that nearly six million employees work at home yet commute to work on a full- or part-time basis by telephone, computer, and other electronic devices. First you telecommute to work as an employee. Then you realize you could be your own boss and do the same work or perhaps change careers and work at home.

I can't help but be amused by the image that so many people have of at-home workers. In the mid-1970s, I relocated my public relations firm to a corporate office building in suburban New Jersey. My fellow tenants included Citibank, N.A., Chase Manhattan Bank, N.A., Chrysler Corporation, Konica Business Machines USA, and Volkswagen of America, Inc.

I was not a career changer at the time, but I was taking the first step in creating a new lifestyle. My office was hardly a domestic setting, yet my telephone callers imagined I was running my firm from home dressed in jeans or, worse yet, my bathrobe. I even got to the point of wanting to tape the sounds of a dishwasher or of a baby crying to complete a caller's false image of the office in the kitchen.

Manages an Investment Portfolio Remotely

Peter DeLisser (early forties) is a beneficiary of computer technology. It enabled him to leave the investment banking department of Morgan Stanley and Company, Inc. in New York City and relocate to Ketchum, Idaho (population 2353).

With direct access to financial data bases, DeLisser manages an $18 million convertible securities portfolio as easily from Idaho as from midtown Manhattan, and more often than not, he leaves work by 2 p.m. to fish, ride horses, and hike. On Sunday mornings, he's the host of a jazz show on a local radio station.

Duplicates Her City Office at Home

Reni Witt (late thirties) is enthusiastic about her ability to work at home. When her son was born in 1989, Reni, an editor who had recently changed careers to become an entrepreneur, reduced her daily railroad commute to once or twice a week.

As the owner of a New York City-based media awards company, she installed a computer, modem, and fax in her at-home office. Her automated home office gives her the flexibility to attend personally to her son as well as manage both office and staff on a remote basis.

A TV Producer Works from Home

Jim Hatfield (late forties) knows what it's like to receive a pink slip. It came at a closed-door meeting with his boss, the station manager of WBBM-TV, a CBS-owned station in Chicago where Jim for 17 years was a producer of a 30-minute weekly public affairs program. His program was canceled because of changing market conditions, and with it went his job and a $96,000 salary.

"After considering looking for a new job for about 10 seconds, I decided to do what I'd always wanted to do anyway—start my own video production company at home. No more corporate cliff-hanging, no more going through channels to reach the CEO. I would be the CEO." Several years later, Hatfield, now busier than ever in his own production company, says his income is approaching his WBBM-TV salary.

Lifestyle was a fundamental part in the formation of Jim Hatfield Productions. It began, as do so many new businesses, on a bridge table in a spare bedroom. One naturally expects a TV newscaster to be au courant when it comes to computer technology, but Jim was indifferent to technical equipment. When the station was converting from manual to electronic typewriters, it took him nearly two years to open the box.

Dissatisfied with this makeshift home office, he took out a loan, built a 600-square foot office, spent about $10,000 on computers, software, and related communications equipment, and taught himself how to operate it.

"The first thing I learned is that people who write for a living need to produce good-looking copy, so I invested in a PC and laser printer. To give myself a competitive edge and to make the most of my broadcast-honed abilities—turning out good copy, fast—I added a fax board."

Jim's office houses both his work and play tools: a trumpet, a cornet, and a flügelhorn. "I can practice jazz licks while I'm waiting for my laser printer to do its stuff...now there's something I couldn't do at CBS."[5]

------------◆------------

Points to Remember

- ▶ Lifestyle is used to describe both work and play.
- ▶ The yuppies and baby-boomers are potentially prime career changers.
- ▶ Moving to a new location isn't always the answer.
- ▶ Top management is still overworked.
- ▶ Money isn't everything.
- ▶ Flexible scheduling is growing slowly.
- ▶ There are advantages to working from home.

------------◆------------

CHAPTER 7

The Hobbyist Goes to Work

We are a nation of hobbyists. We contend that hobbies make life worthwhile, to which career counselor John Liptak adds, "leisure activities can serve as a vocational tryout that allow people to try themselves out in occupationally related activities as a way of testing a career."[1]

Hobbies have become big business among U.S. adults. When the Hobby Industry of America last surveyed the marketplace, in 1990, it noted that at least one family member in 77 percent of U.S. households engages in a minimum of one craft or hobby, a jump of 12 percent over the results of a similar survey conducted two years previously.

The hobby industry is fractionalized. Few companies dominate any segment of the hobby field, yet many niche specialty industries, such as quilting and weaving, produce billion dollar sales. Baseball cards alone now account for over $1 billion in sales, 20 times the sales volume recorded in the mid-1970s.[1]

There comes a time when some hobbyists consider taking a hobby and making it a full-time occupation. Beware. Logic and reason should prevail over emotion. John Liptak's advice notwithstanding and even though piggybacking is an important element in career changing, it's one thing to enjoy carving decoy ducks as a hobby and another matter to want or be able to make a living from it.

Daydreams aside, the hobbyist needs to ask, Do I really want to work all day as a painter, cook, or gardener, and can my hobby pay the bills?

Unless your skills are *exceptional*, it's best to keep a hobby as a hobby. Gilbert Kaplan (late forties) knows firsthand the temptations facing the serious hobbyist. Kaplan, founder and publisher of *Institutional Investor Magazine* and other financial publications, is also a skilled musician with a passion for composer Gustav Mahler.

57

Kaplan mastered the complexities of Mahler's *Resurrection* (Second Symphony) by taking a year off to study conducting. Leading the American Symphony Orchestra in the Second, he received favorable concert reviews. Kaplan, realizing the difficulties of conducting, resisted temptation and remains a publisher.

Above all, Kaplan appreciates the difference between career and hobby. He maintains that "passions should remain passions; otherwise they become a profession," a point supported by career counselor Frank Karputi, who warns clients that a wonderful hobby can be a terrible new career.

Bees Are No Longer Just a Hobby

Until Edward Weiss (early seventies) was in his midforties, he and his wife, Anita, lived in a New York City apartment. When they moved to suburban Connecticut, Anita told Ed that the garden needed pollination, and pollination means bees. This was Ed's introduction to bees and the eventual transformation of a beekeeping hobby into a full-time business.

Starting with one hive, he learned the fundamentals from Edna Erickson, a professional beekeeper, and when she died in 1974, she willed her beekeeping equipment supply company to Ed. By then, the Weisses were maintaining 11 hives. At 55 years of age, Ed had spent 28 years with the same industrial equipment company as vice president for marketing. At the time, he decided it was time to do something different. From the simple desire for bees to pollinate a garden, Ed, the hobbyist, emerged as one of approximately 1500 commercial beekeepers in the United States.

Although he has cut back his work load in recent years, Ed at one time maintained as many as several hundred hives, some up to 50 miles from his home. Depending on harvest conditions, his hives yield from 10,000 to 30,000 pounds of honey a season, which he sells under the name of Wilton Gold. As a former marketer, Ed also appreciates the value of sound promotion. His book, *The Queen and I*, now in its second edition, helps sell his honey.

The Amateur Walker Now Walks for a Living

In 1980, Gary Yanker (early forties) literally walked away from his job as a corporate lawyer. He used his newfound hobby, walking, as the basis to establish a communications company, Walking World. Yanker discovered walking as a way to battle a weight and health problem. He was 60 pounds overweight, smoked two packs of cigarettes a day, and lived an overly sedentary life.

Walking became Yanker's answer to satisfy a need to improve his personal fitness. Walking also became a hobby. He walked rather than use local mass transportation. He walked up to 200 miles a week and then took a year off from his job as a staff lawyer for an advertising agency to further his passion in walking. On a 1200-mile walk, Gary, who also has an MBA in marketing, started to conceptualize how he would use his hobby as the basis of a new career to promote walking.

After returning to New York, he wrote magazine articles on health and fitness and gave demonstrations. Soon Walking World was born as a vehicle to market walking for 55 million non-competitive U.S. walkers (there are 30,000 race walkers). By the mid-1980s, Walking World had become a fully integrated communications company, publishing books, how-to pamphlets, and video and audio cassettes and sponsoring sporting events.[2]

From Bridge Building to Quilting

When John Flynn's (late forties) wife started to take quilting lessons, little did he realize that her hobby would soon become his hobby as well and, a few years later, the basis of his new career.

John's professional training and work for over 20 years was far removed from home crafts. He joined the family's construction business in Billings, Montana when he graduated in the mid-1960s as a civil engineer from Montana State University.

His career change started nearly 20 years later when his wife was learning how to quilt. John also became a quilter. His wife then asked him to make her a quilting frame. In the typical response of a trained engineer, he turned her request into a new product.

Rather than build the cumbersome piece of equipment that is normally used in quilt making, he created a lap-top product. Success with this product led to the formation seven years later of the Flynn Quilt Frame Company.

"When I started to make quilts it was a way to relax, a form of stress relief from the pressures of building bridges and the problems of running a small business," he told *Profiles Magazine*. "Quilting was my way to get out of construction."

Quilting is at least a 400-year-old craft. Of the nearly 14 million people in the United States who do some form of quilting, John aims to sell to those he describes as the nearly 1.5 million serious quilters. What started out as an at-home production shop to make compact quilt frames has now broadened into a direct mail and publishing business.

His one-person business grossed nearly $100,000 in 1991 and will double again in 1992 as John expands into international markets. With the release in mid-1992 of his third book on quilting, publishing has become his largest revenue producer.

The Thoracic Surgeon Turns Art Dealer

Charles Abbott's (midfifties) interest in collecting dates back to his teenage years. Collecting stayed somewhat in the background until he left medicine.

Like so many sons of doctors, medicine was the only career he ever considered. After graduating from Harvard College, he completed his medical degree and residency at Tulane University in New Orleans.

When he returned to New Jersey a cardiovascular surgery specialist, Abbott was married and the father of three children. From 1969 until 1987, he was a partner in a 10-doctor surgical specialty group.

"While I was in my midforties, I began to tire of the hassles in medicine—insurance forms, fear of possible litigation, and working with third-party insurers. It took all the fun out of medicine. I was making a lot of money but my wife and I decided that one of our goals was not to die rich. I did not expect a new career to necessarily provide a large income. If necessary, we could live on savings and investments."

Charles is an inveterate collector who started as a teenager with antique musical instruments. His interest in collecting continued, and in the early 1980s, he began to buy antique botany and children's books. Knowing he wanted to become a professional collector, he established Sudbury Galleries.

He tested the waters during the next few years, and he sent a signal to his medical partners that he was considering doing something else. "When I announced my retirement plans some of my partners were shocked. At my retirement dinner, I advised them that they should also consider changing careers every 25 years."

Sudbury Galleries operates from Abbott's home to avoid being a walk-in retail showroom. He attends book fairs in the United States and Europe and exhibits his nature prints at five or six art shows a year. Like so many career changers, he learns by doing, making mistakes, asking questions, and drawing from his lifelong skills as a collector.

Consistent with their early retirement plan, the proceeds from Sudbury Galleries are reinvested in the business to buy additional books and art. The Abbotts live on income from investments and savings.

From Sporting Goods to Fine Asian Art

Donald Wineman (early sixties) is also a confirmed collector. Stamps were his introduction to collecting.

When Don graduated from St. Lawrence University, his first job was in a department store training program. A few years later he left retailing for what would be a series of marketing jobs in the sporting goods industry. During this period, he started to collect maps and rare books.

Collecting was then only a hobby, but Don picked up experience and made mistakes. He also learned a valuable lesson, one that he would use as a dealer. The items that he wanted to buy were usually expensive. To buy them calls for capital, and when you aren't personally wealthy, a collection needs to generate income continually. This was the case with his collection of Chinese cloisonné. The major collector was an European multimillionaire. When he sold his collection, Don's smaller collection, now doubled in price, was also sold.

When he left the sporting goods business to work full-time as a dealer, Don decided to specialize in fine Asian art objects. In addition to his acquired knowledge, he increased his understanding of Asian art by buying a set of highly valued Asian art books. These books serve as his prime source of information, permitting him to negotiate on a nearly real-time basis on behalf of private collectors as well as major art museums in New York City, Baltimore, Cleveland, and Washington, D.C.

Don's retail training influences his approach to collecting. He adheres to a retailing fundamental that emphasizes the need to turn over merchandise to create capital. Unlike some collectors, he doesn't hoard art objects until he can obtain his price. By generating income, he has the money to buy art. As a result of this sales formula, Don's income exceeds his previous corporate salaries.

———————◆———————

Points to Remember

► The United States is a nation of hobbyists.

► Do you want to earn your living from a hobby?

► The hobby business is big business.

► Will your hobby then turn from pleasure to work?

► Make sure that you can earn a living from a hobby.

► Don't be romantic about your hobby.

———————◆———————

CHAPTER 8

Hanging Up the Uniform

THE MILITARY

Question: Why is September 30, 1995 a significant date?

Answer: By then, the number of men and women on active duty in the military—Army, Navy, Air Force, and Marines—will drop to 1.6 million, or 340,000 less than it was four years earlier. Add to this dropout rate another 121,000 civilian employees of the U.S. Department of Defense along with untold numbers of employees of defense contracting companies. The cutbacks will result mainly from scheduled retirements, attrition, voluntary release, and the introduction of early retirement plans. Even so, where will nearly 460,000 people find employment?

Many departees will compete for jobs in private-sector markets in which civilian layoffs have already been severe. In many ways, women, who were denied military assignments in most combat and high-risk commands, are in a better position to obtain civilian jobs than their male counterparts. Assigned to support units, they have portable skills that are more readily transferable to the civilian data processing, health care and food services, and education and training job market.

Ever since the Vietnam War, the normal policy was to retire on one-half base pay after 20 years of active service. Other than high-ranking officers, the recycling of most other officers and enlisted personnel was orderly, structured, and predictable. Downsizing, a "peace dividend" resulting from the end of the Cold War, has changed the game plan by producing a mass exodus over the next several years.

THE CHALLENGE

The retirement system now works differently. Replacing it is the "copper handshake" severance package, which *Time Magazine* describes as "a staff sergeant with 10 years service can choose to leave with a $28,100 lump-sum payment or a $4,700 annual annuity over 20 years. But, if the same sergeant does not volunteer to retire, he or she can be separated with one-third less pay."

The Route One Officer Took

Leaving the military is one thing; finding a job represents a more formidable challenge. William Houser's military and civilian career could serve as a pattern for other retirees. Houser applies the lessons he learned in making his career change as a template for other military personnel who are about to retire.

Trained at West Point, Bill (late fifties) served in Vietnam, returned to the United States, and was assigned at age 34 to the Pentagon, where he was fortunately assigned to a job in which the work correlated with the civilian job market. Over the next 10 years, his assignment centered on identifying likely junior officers and assigning them to positions with greater responsibility.

He decided to retire at age 47. He reasoned that if he waited a few years longer, he would be too old to find a good civilian job. Unlike many other officers of his rank, he did not want to go the normal retirement route—a job with a defense contractor—or to live in an area with a high concentration of retired military personnel. At the time, his children were college aged and his wife, a fashion designer, wanted to live in an area that would further her career.

Bill evaluated his skills: a master's in history—not sufficient to teach at the university level. To get a doctorate would take another four years. Corporate employment looked more promising. What skills did he have to offer? Those of a combat officer do not translate into the skills needed in industry.

He put himself in the position of potential employers. Never having worked in industry, he would be competing for jobs with men and women who had paid their corporate dues. Looking for work, Bill emphasized the crossover betweeen his military personnel assignment and defined it in terms of the civilian job market.

In his informal talks with retired military personnel, Bill recommends that they be willing to start their new careers at the bottom of the corporate ladder. When they leave the military at 35, he finds that it's not too difficult to take a lower or entry-level position. At 50, the transition is more difficult, especially when you're reporting to someone 20 years younger.

His first job was as an executive assistant to the chairman of a multimedia conglomerate. "I actually was his 'go-fer' and a year later, based on mutual understanding, I left." In 1979, Bill was hired by Pfizer, Inc., an international pharmaceutical company, as director of personnel development, a job that resembled the one he had in the Army.

Some Advice from the Experts

Unlike Bill Houser, who serves as volunteer adviser to military retirees, Stanley Hyman has made his living over the past 23 years counseling approximately 17,000 military personnel about retirement.

For five weeks, one night a week at a cost of $505, he conducts his workshops a few miles from the Pentagon. Hyman doesn't believe that business wants to hire from the military. His mission is to prepare military retirees for the commercial marketplace.

Hyman typically uses humor to instruct military retirees: "Wear a watch with hands. You don't need one that tells time on the moon. And a watch that beeps during an interview is death." Listing two years of mine warfare experience earned one resume unwarranted attention: "We don't use mines in the business world."[1]

Military retirees should recognize a number of the key differences between the military and civilian workplace. The orientation starts with an understanding that one's former military rank has little afterlife in business. Similarly, after 10 or more years of military service, most personnel have lived in a sheltered environment. They need to become familiar with the ways business operates.

"Take courses, speak to civilian friends and family members to find what it's like to work in business" is the way that Roy Ketchum, a retired Army colonel and now a partner in an executive search firm, advises clients.

Retirees with more than 20 years of experience are usually generalists. Ketchum tells clients to look beyond *Fortune* 500 companies and concentrate instead on smaller, less structured companies, who more readily employ jacks-of-all-trades.

This concept is supported by the findings from a survey of 100 smaller employers in New Jersey; 82 percent regard recent veterans as more productive than other hires and also more "team oriented," 74 percent find them easier to train, 56 percent believe their technical skill is superior, and 54 percent would actively recruit discharged veterans *if a job were to become available.*[2]

Military personnel entering the job market differ from other mid-life career changers. Compared with civilian career changers, who mostly flee large companies as part of the career change, military personnel seek them out. As one retired military officer put it, they feel more comfortable in a structured, big-company environment. The recruitment priorities at many larger companies, such as Coors Brewing, Corning Glass International, SA, and GE Company, are veterans with engineering, computer, and other technical skills.

INTO THE CLASSROOMS

Many military retirees are already qualified to teach in the nation's schools. Of those scheduled to leave the Army in the next several years, 20 percent are officers and 99 percent have baccalaureate degrees, says Patricia Hines, the Army's deputy assistant secretary for training and education.

At the rank of major and above, 80 percent have either master's degrees or doctorates. In addition, between 10 and 20 percent of military retirees have engineering backgrounds that would enable them to teach high school physics.[3]

Management and organizational skills are considered assets in teaching careers. Training, a major component of military life, provides a logical bridge to a career in education. Proof of this, says *Industry Week*, is the $21 billion the military spends each year to conduct some 540 schools and 24,000 courses, making it the world's largest school system.

The idea of taking military personnel and encouraging them to become teachers has many supporters. The National Executive Service Corps is one group that has developed programs at several military installations to help prepare Army and Navy personnel for careers in teaching. An NESC-supported program at Fort Bragg, North Carolina trains retirees as math and science teachers for the state's middle and secondary schools.

The program consists of approximately 15 course hours devoted to classroom teaching techniques, compressed into three consecutive eight-week sessions. This is followed by 25 hours of classroom observation but no practice teaching. A retiree is then employed by a North Carolina school as a provisional teacher, and following an internship and three months of monitored classroom teaching, the intern is certified.

The pattern in North Carolina and a few other states is not typical of what's taking place in other areas. Alternative state certification, a flexible system that was devised to bring more midlife career changers into teaching, has been only marginally successful. (Alternative certification is discussed at greater length in Chapter 9.)

Military retirees face the same restrictive employment practices as other midlife career changers seeking teacher certification. As a result of the impasse in becoming certified, the impact of military retirees has been minimal. Since 1987, according to one government estimate, only 2000 to 3000 military retirees have become public school teachers.

POLICE AND FIREFIGHTERS

Compared with downsizing in the military, a more orderly retirement process is in effect for the nation's 280,000 full-time firefighters and 660,000 police. Since 90 percent of firefighters and 85 percent of police work for urban governments, retirement policies are implemented on the local level.

Depending on the local or state contract, police and firefighters normally retire on one-half pay after 20 to 25 years of service.

The Experiences of a New York Cop

The stereotype of retired cops who become security officers and private investigators is changing. John Carlton (late forties), a retired New York City detective, knows better. When he took a disability retirement at age 38 after 18 years of service, John had already planned to retire in another two years.

An active member of New York City's Patrolmen's Benevolent Association, John joined the PBA as an administrator and upon retirement became a career counselor for the nation's largest police union, with 18,000 active and 12,000 retired members. Since then he has completed college, majoring in psychology and minoring in career counseling, two subjects that relate closely to his present career.

"We expect about 800 to 1000 cops to retire each year. They're burned out after 20 years. It's my job to get them ready for their next career. I tell them that they are not retiring, only starting a second career." (John's comments on police retirement in New York City are applicable to most other police departments.)

In the past, a cop's primary objective was to find a job to balance the books. "Now they need a second career and a regular paycheck to meet expenses. Expectations are higher. Children are going to college. A pension of 50 percent of salary is insufficient."

Even though increasingly more cops as well as firefighters have college degrees and some become lawyers, teachers, or nurses or start businesses, most are not prepared for retirement, a problem the PBA addresses by introducing its program about five years before the cop is eligible to retire.

The program, considered a model by police unions in other cities, starts with an annual workshop in which the PBA instructs cops in the ABC's of preparing a resume, job searching, employment opportunities, and handling job interviews. Like the military, police and firefighters need to be oriented to the civilian job market.

The security guard image notwithstanding, the PBA encourages cops to consider jobs in sales, community relations, and human resources. Since the cop's most important job is working with people, the PBA shows how to translate this ability into the civilian job market.

Now Flies Commercial Jets

Laurence Latimer (early forties) is one policeman who planned for his early retirement. Exemplifying the adage, "like father, like son," he has followed in his father's footsteps in many ways as a policeman, pilot, and career changer. Laurence joined the New York City Transit Police in 1969 and retired 20 years later as a sergeant.

"They said I was crazy to retire at the time, since I was only 15 names away from being promoted to a lieutenant." Unlike many other 20-year police and firefighter retirees, Laurence was prepared for the next step. He had planned for his new career for many years.

While a transit cop, Laurence joined the New York Air National Guard and served for 17 years on weekends and vacations as a helicopter pilot. In 1977, he bought a plane with his father. His hobby, flying, became the basis of a second career as an airline pilot.

When he retired in 1989 from the transit police, Laurence, by now a licensed commercial pilot, joined United Airlines as a flight engineer and was promoted to copilot two years ago. (His father, George, is profiled in Chapter 16.)

Once a Fireman, Always a Fireman

Like Joseph Conrad, Dennis Smith (early fifties) never turned his back on his past career. Conrad used 20 years of experience as a sailor and ship's officer as the theme for a number of his novels. Smith, a New York City fireman for 18 years, wrote *Report from Engine Company 82* while still on active duty as a fireman.

When Smith took early retirement, he leveraged his firefighting know-how into a productive second career by writing several more books with a firefighting theme. He also launched and published *Firehouse*, a monthly professional magazine for firefighters.

---◆---

Points to Remember

► Military personnel with portable skills might have an edge in getting a civilian job.

► Many companies seek only technical specialists.

► Generalists shouldn't overlook the smaller companies.

► Military rank carries little weight in the U.S. corporate world.

► Women might have an advantage in finding civilian jobs.

► Police and firefighters should start preparing for retirement years in advance.

---◆---

AND THOSE WHO HAVE DONE IT

Chapters 9 through 12 describe four well-defined professions: education, law, health care (medicine and nursing), and the clergy. Each of these careers has well-defined parameters in terms of specific professional training, certification, and, other than the clergy, state licensing. Accounting, architecture, dentistry, and engineering also fall into this professional classification but were not included in *It's Never Too Late* since they rarely attract career changers.

Even though the number of entrants aged 35 or more into medicine is comparatively low, a larger than average number of career changers take a preliminary look at opportunities in this profession. Interest begins to drop when they learn it takes two to three years for the average career changer merely to prepare for and meet medical school entrance requirements. This process is too long for many career changers.

The scenario is somewhat similar in law, the clergy, and education, in which professional training also restricts the ease of entry. Even so, growing numbers of career changers are entering these fields.

Chapters 9 through 12 are organized to provide readers with an overview of career opportunities, the employment marketplace, tips on entering the field, training, the pay, problems affecting career changers, and issues facing women.

Psychologists and social workers, as described in Chapter 13, receive professional training and certification. Many others engaged in community service work enter the field directly from business or other professions without special training.

Chapters 14 through 17 deal with a different group of career changers, those who seek opportunities as entrepreneurs or in craft fields. These fields are filled with risk takers. The people profiled in these four chapters broke with past careers to enter fields as diverse as merchandising, gourmet cooking, restaurants, bed-and-breakfast inns, wallpapering, cabinetmaking, sculpture, journalism, interior design, farming, landscape gardening, quilting, and arts and crafts, among others.

Degree-granting programs and trade school courses are available, but most entrants acquire their new skills on the job or by adapting past experiences to their new work. Karen Glance and Paul Mayer typify this spirit. Karen applied the skills learned as a Sears Roebuck and Company mass merchandiser in running her small general store in suburban Minneapolis. Paul, who wrote TV's "Ryan's Hope," uses his theatrical know-how to provide psychotherapeutic counseling to writers and artists.

The profiles in the following nine career chapters are structured similarly. They discuss the individual's previous career, education and personal history, reasons for changing careers, how it was accomplished, the new career, how it affected income and personal and family lifestyle, and, last, how past experiences were applied in the new career.

CHAPTER 9

Education

CAREER OPPORTUNITIES

The U.S. public maintains a love-hate relationship with teachers and teaching. We criticize the quality of our schools yet protest the need for higher taxes to attract more qualified teachers. Our mixed feelings about education have apparently hit home.

Teaching continues to attract the lowest academic quadrant of college undergraduates. According to a University of California–Los Angeles survey, aspiring teachers graduate from colleges that are the least prestigious and academically selective.

On a more positive note, a number of programs aim to attract a "new" breed of young, motivated, and qualified teachers. For the past several years, Teach for America has recruited high-achieving college graduates. In an intensive bootcamp summer program where the staff is inculcated with a Peace Corps esprit, Teach for America readies its recruits to teach in disadvantaged inner city and rural school districts.

The National Executive Service Corps has created a range of programs to encourage a different breed of candidates from the other end of the age spectrum to become teachers, mainly corporate executives and professionals nearing retirement and military retirees.

Careers as teachers appeal to young and old alike, and it seems to attract many midlife career changers. A number of schools of education report that upwards of 25 percent of their graduate students are over 30. Many unfortunately never find employment in public education. State certification stands as a formidable barrier. As an alternative, they are being employed by independent and parochial schools in which certification is not a requirement. Although pay scales are usually not as high as in public education, the teaching environment and working conditions, especially in urban areas, are better.

Dr. Helen Freidus, who has chronicled the movement of career changers into education, has classified career changers into several groups: men in their late thirties to early fifties, perceived as children of the 1960s, who started their adult life focused on public service careers but felt peer pressure early to prove themselves by traditional measures of success; women in the same age bracket who were initially motivated by opportunities in the women's movement and used their energies to become trailblazers in the business world; and men in their late forties and early fifties who have taken advantage of early retirement programs or the sale of a business.[1]

THE MARKETPLACE

There are approximately 2.4 million classroom teachers, a situation that will change dramatically by the year 2001, when large numbers of teachers (the baby-boomers), now in their forties and fifties, start to retire.

With a requirement to fill a nearly 1:1 ratio of job openings to candidates, groups like the Educational Testing Service wonder how we'll be able to hire two million teachers to fill labor quotas in such specialty skill areas as mathematics, physical and biologic sciences, foreign languages, special education, and bilingual education. The shortage of science and math teachers alone is so acute that the National Executive Service Corps points out that there are only 1400 replacements for every 18,000 retiring specialists.

Parts of the country are already experiencing a steady decline in new teachers. They have reached the point at which the supply meets only 70 percent of the demand. No where is this better documented than in teacher training, particularly at the undergraduate level, at which 176,000 students received bachelor degrees in education in 1971. This number decreased to 105,000 in 1990.

Teaching is no longer a sinecure. There once was consistency in a teacher's scenario: get a degree, find a job, get tenure, steady income, and good benefits, and retirement will occur 30 years later. Teaching as a profession and education as an institution have changed.

Like most governmental functions, education is subject to budget restraints and community pressures. Many school districts, caught by either declining enrollments or decreasing financial resources, are reducing faculty size.

Inner city and many suburban school districts as well are traumatized by larger classes and demoralized professional staffs.

Urban school violence and the danger of physical harm make it difficult to recruit and retain experienced teachers. Many teachers in urban schools are taking early retirement.

The U.S. Bureau of Labor Statistics expects teacher employment to grow through the year 2005 as enrollment increases and class size declines. By the mid-1990s, job openings should start to accelerate as a large number of teachers in their late forties and fifties start to retire. Taxpayer pressure to reduce government spending could affect employment opportunities. The difficulty that central cities and rural areas face in attracting teachers is expected to continue.

HOW TO ENTER THE FIELD

The two questions most frequently asked by potential career switchers: What shortcuts are open to executives and professionals who want to enter teaching? How does one apply past work experience and college education as a basis of switching into education? There are 50 different answers to these questions. Since states license teachers, 50 different formulas govern certification.

The growing shortage of math and science teachers has accelerated the need to take a fresh look at certification on a state-by-state basis. Starting in the early 1980s, alternative teacher certification became an educational buzz term, providing a practical way, says C. Emily Feistritzer of the National Center for Education Information, to bring bright, educated, life-experienced, eager adults into the teaching profession. The concept has attracted its critics, who consider alternative certification as downgrading the profession or as a "scab" program.

When the shortfall became evident, there was little relaxation of the state certification process until the early 1980s. New Jersey broke the barrier when it introduced alternative certification as a way to attract qualified math and science professionals.

Over the next 10 years, 38 other states adopted various flexible certification standards to attract teachers in science, math, and other specialties. Despite the concern that more lenient rules would produce a deluge of applicants, only about 1 percent of the one million teachers employed in all teaching fields during this 10-year period acquired their jobs as a result of alternative certification.[2]

Because certification is a state function, standardized national alternative certification or guidelines do not exist. Eleven states have led the way with alternative programs designed to attract people to education who have already received a bachelor's degree in fields other than education. Their programs are open to applicants to teach in any subject at any grade level.

Eight more states have introduced alternative certification programs that are more limited in scope. Their intention is to certify and fill teacher shortages only as they occur in primary or secondary schools or in specific academic subjects.

Conversely, the National Center for Education Information, which monitors alternative certification, notes that 19 states have adopted programs with a narrower base. One state goes so far as to "require that an applicant to its alternative certification route have five years prior teaching experience."

Even though 38 states have established some form of alternative certification, the National Center for Education Information finds that very few states have actually designed a certification path specifically for the growing market of adults who already have at least a bachelor's degree and no (or little) formal training in professional education courses yet want to teach.

A few companies have sponsored programs to permit a limited number of employees to become teachers. The Polaroid Corporation and the Digital Equipment Corporation, both based in Massachusetts, have initiated programs that enable a few employees to make the transition from industry to classroom.

Polaroid created cooperative programs with several colleges in the Boston area. The company pays full salary and tuition for one year. During this period, the employee, who is on corporate leave, completes classroom and student teaching requirements and, it is hoped, finds a teaching job. (See the Ronald Burgess and Victor Tucker profiles in this chapter.)

The cost to qualify as a teacher is dictated to a large extent by the expenses associated with meeting state certification requirements. Tuition is considerably less at public colleges. The process, depending on the state, often requires spending six weeks to an entire semester as a student teacher with no pay.

SOCIAL AND PROFESSIONAL OBSTACLES FACING CAREER SWITCHERS

Tenure rules are in flux as the once accepted practice of granting lifelong tenure is redefined. Some school districts are reluctant to grant tenure automatically to every teacher with above average classroom performance and three to five years of employment.

Under pressure to control costs, school systems are moving to eliminate or at least modify tenure, replacing it with more flexible employment contracts.

In finding a job, teachers are free agents who must sell themselves to department heads, principals, human resource personnel, and, in growing numbers of instances, committees of parents and community leaders. Some school districts retain placement agencies to locate and screen job candidates.

Get in shape for classroom duty. Teaching is a physical job; the life of a classroom teacher is hardly sedentary. Forget the teacher stereotypes. What the public does not see is the time required, particularly of new teachers, to organize and prepare lesson plans, lectures, and classwork; to mark papers and write reports; to attend staff meetings and parent conferences; and to take graduate-level college courses.

The realistic workday matches corporate hours. As a general rule, for every hour spent in the classroom, the new teacher should expect to spend another two to three hours in preparation and review.

Differing little from industry, schools are merging or being eliminated to reflect a community's changing demographics. In the simplest terms, this means that career changers face potential "last in, first out" employment practices.

Before accepting a teaching job, do your homework on local teacher employment practices, the area's economics, and the financial health of the local civil service job market.

Don't think that leadership skills acquired in business or the military necessarily carry over into teaching. Some career changers have difficulty working with younger supervisors. Others, most notably retired military personnel, often find classroom informality far different from the discipline of the armed forces.

THE WOMEN'S ISSUE

Women should not be overjoyed with what at first appear to be strong comparative statistics in favor of their gender: they only tell one part of the story.

Parity for women still does not exist in education, especially when school administration is a career changer's objective. Men still receive the bulk of upper-echelon supervisory jobs. Although progress is being made, relatively few women are principals of

Bachelor of Education (BEd)		
1971	176,614	75 percent women
1988	87,115	No change

Master of Education (MEd)		
1971	88,952	56 percent women
1988	75,501	74 percent women

Doctor of Education (EdD)		
1971	6,402	21 percent women
1988	3,820	55 percent women

large urban or suburban high schools or administrators of metropolitan school systems.

THE PAY

Don't expect to become rich even though salaries rose $5000 on average, to $31,315, between 1985 and 1990. The salary differential that once existed between secondary and primary grades has nearly disappeared. Career changers who find jobs in independent schools can expect to earn less than entry-level teachers in public institutions.

A total of 30 states have implemented minimum entry-level salaries, with 15 states plus the District of Columbia mandating a $20,000 minimum salary. The list consists of the more populated states—California, Florida, New Jersey, New York, Pennsylvania, and Texas. New teachers, reports the National Center for Eduation Statistics, nationally averaged $20,476 in 1990, the latest year of record. The minimum entry-level salary in California is $22,780 compared with $15,290 mandated in South Dakota.

Teachers are generally better paid in the Northeast, Middle Atlantic, and Pacific Coast states. Southern, southwestern, the less populated midwestern states, and parochial and private schools have lower pay scales. Since salaries normally follow the availability of funds, wealthier suburban and large metropolitan school districts usually pay more than rural and economically depressed areas.

THE CAREER SWITCHERS

From Four-Engine Jets to the Classroom

Thomas Hosterman (late fifties) retired 22 years and 22 days after joining the U.S. Air Force. No sooner had he graduated from high school, Tom joined the Air Force as an enlisted man, rising to master sergeant. Attending officer's candidate school as a "mustang" (the military term for an officer without a college degree), Tom was commissioned, trained as a multiengine pilot, and served several overseas tours in Japan and Vietnam.

Although he was on the promotion list for lieutenant colonel, Tom retired as a major at age 39 while stationed at Pope Air Force Base in North Carolina. Retirement was hardly a surprise to his family because it was never his intention to serve 35 years. His father was a teacher, as were eight aunts and uncles; Tom's grandfather taught for 60 years.

"Why retire when you're too old to do something else? I found my inspiration in the Air Force service. I knew I wanted to teach high school when I saw a 35 percent dropout rate in pre-flight school due to poor math skills."

Tom's retirement gave him the time to go to college and train for a second career as a teacher. He had some equivalency credits, and by taking 27 points a semester, he completed a three-year academic program in 16 months. Because his course load exceeded the limitations at Fayetteville State University, he also attended North Carolina State University in Raleigh. Typically he got up at 5 a.m., drove 57 miles in the morning to class in Raleigh, ate lunch in his car while listening to lecture tapes, went to class in Fayetteville, and returned home for dinner. He studied in the backyard in a trailer set up to assure privacy.

Except for a four-year period in the late 1970s when he was an assistant high school principal, Tom taught math at the secondary level for more than 15 years. Unlike other military retirees, Tom found little difficulty switching from the armed forces to the relaxed give-and-take atmosphere of the classroom. "It's easy to rate your classroom accomplishments. In the Air Force, an officer is saluted based on rank and guaranteed respect; as a teacher, the students make the final decision. One year I received 93 Christmas cards from my students."

His teaching career ended in 1991; it lasted almost 20 years, nearly as long as his Air Force career. In addition, Tom has now achieved financial independence with dual military and North Carolina pensions.

The Transition of a Former Biochemist

Henry Oliver (midfifties) grew up in the segregated South, where, despite the racial injustices, he received an excellent education. Henry graduated near the top of his St. Petersburg high school class and was the first person in his family to go to college. He was already midway through Hampton College in Virginia in 1954 when the Supreme Court declared segregation in the public schools to be unconstitutional.

Henry majored in both biology and education at Hampton, very much aware that a research or scientific career in science was off-limits for most African-Americans. As a counterpoint, students at black colleges usually took teacher training along with their primary major. In Henry's case, this would provide him with the credentials at least to teach science.

When he graduated from Hampton, employment discrimination was rampant, especially in scientific and technical companies. They did little or no recruiting from black colleges. Drafted into the army, he was stationed at Brooke Medical Center in San Antonio, an assignment that kindled an interest in microbiology. Besides gaining confidence in his scientific skills, he found that he was accepted as a professional; color was secondary.

Returning to civilian life, Henry worked eight years as a microbiologist for several pharmaceutical companies. He was distressed with the segregated corporate lifestyle and disturbed that he was moving further away from his ambition to teach at the university level.

When the Caldwell, New Jersey school system advertised that it was looking for a high school science teacher, Henry applied and was hired for $9000 (an accepted entry-level salary for teachers in 1967), equal to what he was earning as a Warner-Lambert Company researcher. His star began to shine. He integrated real-life science applications into the classroom, sharing 11 years of laboratory experience with his students. "Hospitals gave me rats, hamsters and other specimens to use in experiments. I created a new science program." One of only three African-Americans among the 250 Caldwell teachers, Henry, as in the army 10 years earlier, was treated as a professional, not a black professional.

Talent finds its own level, and Henry was no exception. Montclair, another although larger New Jersey suburban community, hired him as an assistant high school principal, and for the next 16 years he held a series of administrative positions in the Montclair school system. Even as an administrator and with a doctorate in educational leadership, Henry never lost his interest in science. As principal of a middle school, he built a planetarium in Montclair and used it in conjunction with a space training program conducted by the National Aeronautics and Space Administration.

After leaving Montclair, he became assistant superintendent of schools for the Englewood, New Jersey school system, and a few years later was promoted to superintendent. As an administrator, Henry's concern for a more active science curriculum continues. "As in the past, I borrow from what I learned as a microbiologist by creating programs that combine academics with real-life scientific experiments."

Took 20 Years to Make the Change

June Belk's (midforties) decision to exchange an $83,000 job for a $21,000 a year teaching assignment actually germinated 20 years earlier when she was a University of Texas student. Instead of becoming a teacher, she was recruited by Rockwell International Corporation as a management trainee.

"It was the late 1960s and Rockwell wanted to put more women into the workforces," Instructor Magazine reported. "They told me if I went to work for them, they'd train me to be a manufacturing engineer. Not only was the money 50 percent more than I would be making in teaching, if I succeeded I'd become one of the few women manufacturing engineers in the country."

Even her professional success at Rockwell wasn't sufficient to dissuade June from returning to a lifelong dream of being a classroom teacher. While at Rockwell, her assignments brought her closer to the classroom as she moved from industrial engineering to human resources. As a corporate administrator, June had the opportunity to polish her stand-up teaching skills. "Well in advance of the career switch, I got my life in order. I saved money and downscaled my living expenses."

The protocol for career switchers to qualify in Texas for alternative teacher certification is comparatively simple: to be eligible for employment, the applicant needs a bachelor degree and three months of intensive practice teaching, along with two graduate courses in the subject to be taught. The next hurdle is finding a job. When June looked for work, she was selected from among 1200 alternative certification teachers applying for 60 openings.

June enthusiastically entered the classroom, but reality set in no sooner than she was assigned as a reading specialist in a Houston middle school. She found that corporate training differed from classroom teaching. "When Rockwell provided job training, employees listen. Their immediate jobs depend on learning new work skills but in the classroom there is too much apathy from both the kids and their parents. Some students bring neither pens or papers to school, ignore homework or sleep through class. It was up to me to motivate my students and it was my responsibility as their manager to redirect them."[3]

Corporate Trainer Enters the Classroom

Until he became an intermediate school reading teacher in Uxbridge, Massachusetts, Ronald Burgess (midfifties) held a series of jobs as a mailman, sign painter, store clerk, and draftsman and then, for more than 15 years, as a Polaroid training specialist.

He received a degree in elementary education from Providence College when he was in his early thirties, but the practicalities of supporting five children meant deferring a teaching career for a higher paying job in industry. Years later, Ron was finally able to act upon his dream when he became a member of the first group of Polaroid employees to participate in the company's one-year subsidized teacher-training program. While Polaroid paid the tuition and his $38,000 a year salary, he completed a master's program at Leslie College in Boston and worked four months as a student teacher.

Employed initially as a middle school teacher and then reassigned to the primary level, Ron, like June Belk, is somewhat dismayed by the classroom scene.

"At Polaroid, I worked for the training department. I taught technicians how to assemble a camera or a computer. They pay attention to what's being taught since they get paid on the basis of learning new techniques. Not so in schools, and especially in a mill town like Uxbridge, where education is important but not a critical factor."

Ron had to overcome his students' basic indifference by applying lessons learned as a Polaroid trainer. Although he is a product of a more disciplined parochial school education, he adapts a flexible attitude in teaching reading to youngsters who basically do not see its importance. As an alternative tactic, he created the nonbook book report.

"Kids get sick of book reports. Having read a book, a student can use the characters, the plot, the text to construct TV-styled interviews, comic books or picture collages, a mental process similar to writing a book report."

Like so many teachers, Ron is feeling the stress of tightening fiscal controls and potential layoffs. Earning $14,000 less than his Polaroid salary and teaching reading rather than elementary education, he is already considering the next phase in expanding his teaching capabilities. "I got my undergraduate education on the GI Bill and a master's from Polaroid. Who's going to pay for a doctorate?"

An Early Retiree Teaches Trade School

Victor Tucker's (early sixties) education stopped at the twelfth grade. Starting with service in the Navy as an electrician during the Korean War, Victor was a technician before the advent of solid-state technology. The next 40 years were spent as an electrician and foreman. Even so, Victor has been a vocational teacher for the past several years in a suburban Boston regional high school. Like Ron Burgess, Victor made his changeover with the help of Polaroid.

When Polaroid unveiled its early retirement plan in the late 1980s, Victor moved quickly. "Why not a teacher? I've had nine children and have coached baseball, hockey, and basketball. I always wanted to teach, and Polaroid gave me the chance to use 40 years' experience in a different way. If anything, I know how to motivate kids."

Massachusetts permits and, in fact, encourages skilled technicians to teach vocational and trade skills and does not require a bachelor degree. Victor took the mandatory 18 hours of course credits necessary to qualify for a vocational teacher's certificate. As a classroom teacher, his combined pension and salary surpass the $40,000 he earned at Polaroid.

The Blue Hill Regional High School curriculum blends classroom theory with hands-on training, a concept that complements Victor's real-life work experiences. Under his direction, students do nearly all the electrical repair for the school, working with state-of-the-art equipment in a modern building.

"What I really like is their attitude. There are few classroom problems, and absenteeism is low. Unlike many students in traditional academic high schools, vocational students come to school to learn a trade. They pay attention since they know their schoolwork will put money in the bank when they graduate."

From the Research Lab to the Ivy League

Richard Golden (early sixties) lives the corporate executive's dream as a result of fortuitous networking. At 56, Dick, a Princeton

University PhD in chemical engineering, took early retirement from ARCO Chemical Company, where he was vice president for research and development. Although he was under no immediate pressure to retire, he saw the handwriting on the wall. Dick found ARCO's financial package too tempting to resist.

He spent 30 years in industry, most of it as a research and development manager. Dick's career was capped during the last six years, when he directed ARCO's $25 million research budget and a staff of 200 professionals. Throughout his career, he never flirted, as many scientists do, with academia. Although he associated with a number of colleges on technical projects, his career focused on industrial applications.

After leaving ARCO, Dick for the first time in his career was unemployed. Assigned as an outplacement client to Drake Bean Morin, Inc., he ultimately was employed by the firm to advise other engineers and scientists who were outplacement clients.

"I don't know how long I would have stayed at Drake Bean. Though I found many parts of the job enjoyable, there was a certain sameness to the work. As a corporate manager, I was used to more activity."

From a notice in Princeton University's weekly bulletin, Dick learned that the School of Engineering was looking for an associate dean to handle all nonacademic functions. Even with his lack of university teaching and related administrative experience, Dick believed the job approximated those he held in corporate management. To get the Princeton job, however, Dick had 19 separate interviews in four months.

"If anything, I learned patience. I was questioned about my age but I assured questioners that at 59 I was not going to be doing any future job hopping. Some faculty members objected to a nonacademic, corporate executive becoming an associate dean. Even so, I was selected on the basis of my corporate experience."

Joining the administration in early 1990, Dick has not become victim to the plight that hinders so many other corporate converts to academia. They attempt to apply business know-how in their new setting yet fall short in their ability to get things done. They never fully understand how universities operate. Dick realized that managerial techniques in industry do not automatically apply in a college, where there is little line authority. Fortunately, when he was a corporate executive, he managed on the basis of consensus, a technique he uses at Princeton.

The Advantages of Strong Mathematical Skills

When Richard Marx (late fifties) was a high school student, his algebra teacher was also his guidance counselor. Based on his strong mathematical skills, he was advised to train for a career as an actuary. Nearly 40 years later, Dick still credits math for launching his second career.

After graduating from the University of Pennsylvania Wharton School of Finance, Dick, the math major, joined Mutual of New York and spent the next 31 years as a MONY actuary. When he took early retirement, he was an assistant vice president. Dick applied actuarial skills to planning the financial feasibility of his own retirement.

"I made lots of calculations, projected them out, and, based on the facts, I decided on early retirement. I ruled out finding another job as an actuary. I always considered teaching as my second career, but I thought it would take place at 65 rather than 55."

Dick qualified for a New York State teaching certificate when he completed mandated student teaching requirements and a Master of Education degree. Then his problems started. The national shortage of math teachers aside, the local job market, even in his specialty, was lean.

As an alternative, Dick became a part-time math teacher at two local colleges and Keio High School, a private school, which offers a curriculum matching the academic standards of Keio University in Japan. In 1991, he joined the Keio faculty as a full-time algebra and computer sciences teacher.

As one trained in mathematical accuracy, Dick evaluates his transition from actuary to classroom teacher with equal precision. "I know how to integrate the theoretical and practical. I show students how to use math to solve actual problems."

From Sales to the Classroom

Like Richard Marx, "Lynn Weston" (not her real name; late thirties) worked for only one company until she decided it was time for a change in careers.

Lynn, like many other English majors, went to work in advertising when she graduated from college. For the next 13 years, she was employed by a large advertising agency in account management. "When I graduated from college, I was unsure about my career. I didn't consider teaching then, and I doubt if I could have stood the rigors of the classroom at 22."

Lynn left her advertising agency job when she found the work no longer challenging and that her professional priorities had changed. She completed an accelerated accreditation program and was hired as an English teacher in a suburban middle school. A year after her career change, Lynn, now with a Master of Education degree, was earning $30,000, far short of her former salary in advertising.

"As a teacher, I feel less political pressure than in business. It's more like being a free agent. I like the direct ties with the kids, getting them to write properly. Unlike business, there is hardly ever a dull day. There's no such thing as repetition in teaching, to the point that I'm spending three hours a night and Saturday and Sunday preparing. I admit part of the heavy work load results from being a new teacher, but even so it's like preparing in business every day for five separate meetings or corporate presentations."

A Husband and Wife Team

In high school in West Virginia, Rand Jarrell (midforties) excelled in debate. He liked the concept of winning an argument, to the point that advocacy formed the basis of becoming a lawyer. When he was in his early thirties, Rand moved to Anchorage, Alaska in search of a new lifestyle and an opportunity to build a tax law practice.

His practice succeeded. In less than 10 years, he ranked in the top 5 to 10 percent of the lawyers in Alaska in terms of income. Rand enjoyed working with clients who were mostly wealthy, self-made entrepreneurs. Although attracted initially to law by what Rand describes as "the clash of ideas," he began to find the daily practice of law somewhat unimaginative. Working as much as 75 to 80 hours a week, he found legal practice too time-consuming. Even with a solid legal practice, Rand had not forgotten his goal to stop practicing law while still young enough to train for other work.

Rand's wife, Diane (also midforties), a telephone company service and marketing executive for 10 years, actually provided the career-switching incentive. Diane, also from West Virginia, met Rand when they were both Marshall University undergraduates.

Diane majored in education and always wanted to be a teacher. When they moved to Washington, D.C. while Rand was attending law school, there was a local glut of teachers. With 1000 applicants applying for the same job, Diane, for the sake of expediency, became a businesswoman.

Unlike other women graduates in the late 1960s who deliberately avoided teaching, she had an unwritten understanding with Rand that she would eventually become a teacher. The opportunity presented itself nearly 11 years later when their son was in his midteens. She resigned her telephone company marketing job, and without the required certification needed to teach in Alaska's public schools, she obtained a private school teaching job.

By the time their son completed high school in 1984, she had decided that a master degree was necessary to teach gifted students. There was one hitch: Alaska offered no suitable Master of Education program. Diane enrolled at the University of Denver, and the day her son left home as a freshman to attend the University of Oregon, Diane boarded another flight for Colorado.

Rand, mostly out of curiosity, decided to learn about Diane's work so he'd at least be more conversant. He took several weekend courses given in Alaska by one of Diane's Denver professors who was on loan to the Alaska school system.

"I sniffed the glue and I liked the smell. And, like Diane, I became interested in teaching gifted kids."

Rand took three months to liquidate his firm and assets in anticipation of a career switch and move to Denver to qualify for certification in his specialty. By this time, Diane had already received a MEd and was teaching in Denver.

In some ways Rand's timing was bad. He disposed of his Alaskan assets during a falling real estate market, "I even weighed the possibility of returning to Alaska to restore some of my lost equity, but I decided to make the career move regardless of the investment loss."

Diane and Rand started the next leg in their career change in 1987, when they became doctoral students at Teacher's College in New York. They both wanted to teach the gifted, but they also wanted to avoid a possible job conflict. They lessened this possibility by specializing academically and professionally in different areas related to gifted children.

Two people in the same family studying over a five-year period for doctoral degrees presents a financial challenge. They relied on fellowships and grants, faculty housing, savings, and paid positions as administrators in programs for gifted students to pay tuition and New York City living expenses.

The Jarrells specified a number of career and personal objectives when they left Alaska. One was to relocate to a warmer climate, preferably Arizona or New Mexico. When they completed their doctorates, they met all their goals but one. They remained in New York. Diane is a staff member in a school for the gifted, Rand an assistant professor of early childhood development at a local college.

---◆---

Points to Remember

► A number of programs exist to attract career changers.

► Certification is a thorny issue.

► Be aware of the downside to alternative certification.

► There is an ongoing need for math and science teachers.

► Tenure is not easy to achieve.

► The pay scale is improving.

► Women may dominate in the classroom, but the scenario differs in administration.

---◆---

CHAPTER 10

Health Care

CAREER OPPORTUNITIES AS A DOCTOR

If you're looking for controversy, ask your doctor friends how they feel about "over 40 year plus" medical school students. Don't expect too charitable a reply. Although these doctors won't question their sincerity, many disparage their social value as physicians considering they have fewer years of professional service. This commentary notwithstanding, a career change to medicine is at best a difficult task.

Although career-changing opportunities exist in public health, occupational and physical therapy, and medical technology, this chapter focuses primarily on medicine and nursing.

THE MARKETPLACE

The nation's annual health care bill is nearing $750 billion a year, double what it was in the mid-1980s. It accounts for the largest percentage and actual dollar expenditure in the gross national product.

The demographics of the medical profession are worth noting: 615,000 of the nation's medical doctors, based on a 1990 American Medical Association study, are distributed among 38 different board-certified specialties; 3 of 10 doctors work in general and family practice and internal medicine; about 60 percent are in either solo or group practice; and the balance work as hospital staff or in the armed forces, public health clinics, and health maintenance organizations.

The highest ratio of physicians to the population is in the Northeast, the lowest in the South. Rural and blighted urban centers have difficulty attracting doctors.

Osteopathic doctors are located primarily in states that have osteopathic hospitals. Of the 32,000 osteopathic doctors,

80 percent practice in 15 states, with the largest concentrations in Michigan, Florida, New Jersey, Ohio, Pennsylvania, and Texas.

Medical school enrollment mirrors general trends in our society. The twin effects of the economic downturn and corporate downsizing have helped to stimulate the number of older medical school applicants. Admission officers anticipate that this trend will continue.

In 1981, only 35 people over age 37 entered medical school; nine years later there were 180 students, a 500 percent rise. In the class of 1994, 4.4 percent, or 637 matriculants, are age 32 to 37, compared with 2.4 percent, or 405 matriculants, in the early 1980s. As a point of reference, the Association of American Medical Colleges refers to students over 28 as "older students."

Unlike younger medical school students, older students are aware that their age may present some professional problems. In planning their medical careers, I found that students 35 and older are often encouraged to specialize in primary health care services, such as internal medicine, family practice, and geriatric medicine. Besides the general shortage and demand for these basic medical skills, hospital residencies take half the time of other medical specialties.

Older medical students, 35 and over, want to get out and start practicing medicine as quickly as possible, a finding with which *Medical Economics Magazine* agrees. In its survey, it indicated that the average retirement age for physicians is 65. An exception exists for emergency room doctors, who tend to retire earlier, at age 61, and psychiatrists, who leave the profession at age 70.

Because of the continued expansion of the health care industry, employment opportunities for physicians remain higher. There is an ongoing need to attract more physicians to rural areas and poorer inner city communities. Similarly, some health care analysts believe that there is job saturation in some medical specialties.

Unlike their predecessors, a growing number of newly trained doctors prefer to work in group practices, clinics, and health maintenance organizations and on hospital staffs. This trend is furthered to some extent by an opportunity for closer peer relationships and the availability of more costly equipment. Some physicians select salaried positions because they cannot afford the high costs of setting up a private practice while paying off student loans.

HOW TO ENTER THE FIELD

There are few, if any, shortcuts in the medical school application process. The 33,600 applicants of all ages who competed in 1991 for 16,000 openings in the nation's 126 accredited medical colleges had to meet similar academic standards. All were required to take undergraduate courses in physics, biology, inorganic and organic chemistry, and calculus.

Even with definitive academic requirements and standards, medical schools seek student diversity. Mandatory science courses aside, the history or English literature student is just as welcome an applicant as the zoology major. Some undergraduate colleges have already adapted curriculums to reflect the need to prepare doctors with broader perspectives. Davidson College in North Carolina instituted a medical humanities program that includes courses in genetics, bioengineering, and health technologies.

Career changers, however, face an additional challenge. Other than applicants who have worked in or taught science, most career changers need to take or retake science and related prerequisite courses. In addition, the Medical College Admission Test, better known as the MCATs, is required by nearly all medical schools. Of particular interest to career changers is that medical schools are more concerned with the results of just-completed preparatory courses and MCATs than academic records from the 1970s.

Recognizing the educational needs of career changers, approximately 35 colleges and universities (up from 10 programs in 1986) offer specialized postbaccalaureate, premed programs to teach core science and related laboratory courses as well as provide an academic and advisory platform to help applicants qualify for medical school.

Some "predoc" programs are geared to working students; others require students to spend an academic year on campus. The students range in age from their mid- to late twenties to their midfifties.

Columbia University's postbaccalaureate premed program, the nation's oldest and perhaps largest predoc program, accepts students on a rolling basis for its fall, spring, and winter semesters. Classes are held in the late afternoons and early evening so that they do not conflict with a student's full-time job. As with most predoc programs, it takes on average two to three years from entry to medical school admission. Tuition for the 1992–1993 academic year was nearly $500 a point.

Bryn Mawr College (suburban Philadelphia) started its program in 1972. It accepts up to 55 students. Unlike Columbia, where students combine premed programs with full-time jobs, Bryn Mawr's program is full-time and permits students to complete their requirements in approximately one-half the time. Although Bryn Mawr is a women's college, the program is coeducational. Tuition is $2050 for each course; Bryn Mawr alumnae receive a 50 percent discount.

A relative newcomer, Ohio State University in Columbus started its predoc program in 1990. Unlike many other premed programs, which are conducted by liberal arts colleges, the medical school is the sponsor. State residents pay $900 a semester, out-of-staters, $2500. The program is adapted to the needs of full- and part-time students.

Academic qualifications aside, career changers face other problems in applying to medical school. Many are married with families, and personal obligations directly influence medical school selection.

Career changers should also expect that the older they are, the more difficult the admission process. This is never stated officially, but age is a deterring factor. Applicants who are 35 plus should apply to medical schools that tend to accept a proportionally greater number of nontraditional students.

Other barriers exist. Admission staffs attempt to eliminate dilettantes and romantics. As with candidates of all ages, they look for dedication. Be prepared to demonstrate the reasoning behind the transition from another field into medicine. They're on the lookout for "rebound applicants," those who have been fired or are dissatisfied with a corporate job.

Admission officers don't believe that divine intervention motivates career change. Why medicine at age 38? Where's the professional commitment? To demonstrate commitment, some medical schools recommend that career changers, as well as younger applicants, work as volunteers in a hospital or health care facility.

Medical school tuitions range from $22,000 plus a year at private medical schools (less than one-half of the 127 medical schools are privately owned) to free tuition at California's several state medical colleges.

Tuition at other state medical schools ranges from $2000 to over $7000 per academic year. Scholarships, fellowships, and loans are available to help make a medical education somewhat more affordable. Most career changers by virtue of age do not qualify for combined MD/PhD programs or a tuition-free armed forces or National Health Service Corps medical education.

Very few students hold full-time jobs (see the Jack Berdy profile in this chapter) or simultaneously attend law or business school. Medical schools caution students about conflicting academic and professional commitments.

SOCIAL AND PROFESSIONAL OBSTACLES FACING CAREER SWITCHERS

Medical school is a mental and physical grind. Predoc courses and exposure to hospital life through part-time or volunteer work are at best scant introduction to what lies ahead. Medical school competition is rigid. You'll be competing against men and women who have just completed undergraduate college. Their academic skills will be sharp.

Because they are in better academic shape, younger students usually outperform older career changers scholastically in the first two years. Little wonder that career changers find their first two years in medical school a difficult period of adjustment. Later in their medical training, the pendulum often swings in their favor.

In the third and fourth years, many career changers hit full stride. Older and usually more mature, they relate more easily to real-life medical and hospital conditions.

Medical training means setting new personal priorities. In addition to a strain on financial resources, which is offset by student loans and fellowships, social pressures develop. Older, married students find that medical school ends nearly all nonessential social relationships.

Medical school is also physically demanding. Simply stated: Get in shape. Some medical school administrators said they were concerned about whether some of their older students could meet the stressful demands of four years of medical school followed by a three- to six-year residency.

A doctor's duties go well beyond their medical specialty. Doctors are also administrators who deal with government bureaucracy, insurance companies, medical liability, and associated problems that were considered minor aggravations a decade ago.

Like the police who ticket a speeding driver and then spend hours in court supporting their action, doctors devote increasingly

longer hours to what they believe are nonproductive administrative functions.

THE WOMEN'S ISSUE

The medical profession was at one time completely dominated
by men. At a recent dinner, I sat next to a 70-year-old woman
physician. When I asked her about the composition of her medical
school class in the early 1940s, she said she was one of only two
women students, an unfavorable imbalance that prevailed for
women for another 30 years.

The disparity is apparent; only 6000 of the 81,500 doctors between 55 and 64 years of age are women. A generation later, as
medical schools "opened" their doors, the ratio, according to the
American Medical Women's Association, started to improve:
37,000 of 141,000 physicians under 35 are women. In 1970, 9 percent of U.S. medical students were women; 20 years later this increased to 37 percent.

Don't be misled by the statistical acceleration. Men still
dominate medicine. Differing little from corporate and the other
U.S. professions, women have not as yet moved into commensurate positions of authority on hospital medical staffs, medical
schools, or the administration of health care groups.

The health care profession continues to be essentially sex
segregated: 84 percent of physicians are male and 97 percent of
nurses are female. Medical school administration is even less
representative. Of the 127 accredited U.S. medical schools, there
is not a single woman dean. Women comprise only 2 percent of
the department heads and 21 percent of their faculties.

Discrimination often occurs when applying to medical school.
Even with the current employment laws, married and single
mothers are asked about their family lives, a question that is rarely asked of a middle-aged father appearing before the same admissions committee. Who's going to take care of the children?
What does your husband think of your going to medical school?

THE PAY

Some career changers enter medical school with strong financial
resources. For most, the financial strain doesn't ease significantly until they complete their residencies 7 to 10 years later. Medical

schools advise prospective students to get their houses in order by modifying living standards and reducing, if not totally eliminating, debt.

Much has been written about a doctor's accumulated educational debt. At one medical college, approximately 79 percent of the graduating class incur debt ranging from $5000 to more than $80,000. These figures are consistent with studies that show that 79 percent of medical students nationally accumulate over $48,000 in debt.

With the completion of medical school, the new doctor starts to earn some income. A nationwide average for first-year interns, prepared by Cornell Medical College, shows that starting salaries for interns was $27,122, rising slightly to $34,521 on completion of a six-year residency.

As practicing physicians, income starts to rise and is influenced to a large extent by the medical specialty, the type of practice (solo, group, hospital, health maintenance organization, or government), sex, and geographic location of the practice.

Based on its latest salary survey in late 1990, *Medical Economics* reported that orthopedic surgeons had net incomes of $237,120 a year, the profession's highest, compared with general practitioners, at the other end of the scale at $90,910. As a profession, physicians earn $141,720, surgical specialists earn $198,650, and nonsurgical specialists net $68,230 less, or $130,420.

There is a differential between the earnings of comparable men and women physicians. Medical training completed, the pocketbook takes over.

As in many fields, women physicians earn about one-third less than their male counterparts. A recent salary survey conducted by the American Medical Women's Association showed that the average net income of men with one to four years of experience was $110,600 and women with the same experience made $36,400 less. The difference increases with age. Women physicians with 10 to 20 years of experience earn $99,400 compared with the $158,800 for men.

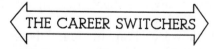

THE CAREER SWITCHERS

From Nurse to Psychiatrist

When Margaret Spinelli (midforties) was director of obstetrics and gynecology nursing at Long Island College Hospital, she learned a valuable professional lesson. No matter how qualified she was as a nurse, the medical doctor was always in charge.

Recognizing the dilemma is one matter. Being able to act upon it is something else. Margaret, a certified nurse with over 12 years of hospital experience and a single parent with 10- and 12-year-old sons, was also completing an undergraduate degree in psychology. While working at a teaching hospital, Margaret met with the dean of the Downstate Medical College to get his views on becoming a doctor.

"In addition to the expected professional questions, he played the devil's advocate, making me face the tough personal problems ahead. How would I support myself and take care of my two sons? What effect would the demands of medical school have on the kids? After more questioning, he suggested that, if I was still interested in medicine, then I should take Columbia's predoc program."

As the first step, she attended Columbia while she worked in medical research. Then came the difficult part. Margaret applied to 20 different schools and was invited for only five interviews. At 35, she had doubts about whether she would be accepted to any school. A few admission committee members even queried her on her ability as a single mother and about the potential difficulties in raising two sons. She had already arranged for them to live with their father, a New York City policeman.

"I got into Cornell. From my first day, I felt lucky to be there. It was hard financially, but I was helped by scholarships, loans, and the availability of low-cost student housing. Even so, I thrived. When you know you're a captive for four years, as you are in medical school, there is only one thing to do and that is totally concentrate on the work to be done. Other than seeing my sons on weekends, I had no other social life. I even gave up writing poetry."

From the start, the advantages of being a nurse were clear. She knew how to be part of a medical team. She could readily relate to doctors. When fellow students were learning new skills, she already knew how to draw blood and take blood pressure. She could relate more easily to patients than many of the younger students.

Academically, however, Margaret found the first two years of medical school particularly difficult. In the third and fourth years, however, when she was assigned to different medical departments, she won honors in seven specialties. After graduating from Cornell in 1988 and completing a four-year psychiatric residency at the New York Hospital–Cornell Medical Center Payne Whitney Psychiatric Clinic, Margaret was accepted to a two-year post-doctoral program at Columbia's Presbyterian Medical Center.

From College Professor to Geriatric Medicine

No sooner had Blanche Skurnick (midforties) received her Columbia University doctorate in eighteenth and nineteenth century British and American literature than she joined the faculty of the City College of New York. During the next 15 years, she became a tenured associate professor in the literature department.

"I knew that I didn't want to teach all my life, and I surely didn't want to write another book. At times, instead of reading humanity publications, I read the *Journal of the American Medical Association*. Yet this was not entirely inconsistent. When I was younger, I wanted to be a doctor. As I grew older, I found it was time to return something to society."

Blanche, by now in her late thirties, had no current premed academic credits. The fun started. After teaching an English class, she would change into jeans and attend a City College chemistry or biology class. Colleagues in the English department had no idea that she was also a premed student, nor did the science faculty know where she worked. They discovered her professional identity when she walked in the academic procession at graduation as a member of the English department faculty.

When applying to medical school, she found that admission officers were pleased with her diverse academic background. Blanche, who lived in suburban New Jersey, was geographically restricted to attending a medical school in the metropolitan New York area. She was able to leave her $40,000 job since her husband's salary would cover her expenses at New Jersey's University of Medicine and Dentistry.

"Medical school was a treat in self-esteem. Of the 200 students in my class, 25 of them, like myself, were black, and there was a proportionately large number of black faculty members. Being an academic, I knew how to study. My years of teaching taught me to explain everything in detail, a skill I carried into medicine."

As a practicing physician, Blanche continues to apply to her patients the methodology she used as an English professor. "I tell them what I'm doing, then what is happening and finally show them how they're doing."

When Blanche completes a joint internal medicine and geriatric residency in the mid-1990s, she plans to practice in an urban area where there is the greatest need for medical help. She finds that the poor too often lack the education to find out for themselves about their health. It's here that she expects once again to find that her teaching skills will prove to be a decided advantage.

The Wife of a Doctor Takes Her Turn

Sally Cohen's career in internal medicine as a partner in a group practice in Ridgewood, New Jersey differs from the midcareer entry by either Margaret Spinelli or Blanche Skurnick. Sally (late forties) never had a nine to five job until she entered medical school 11 years ago.

When she was an undergraduate, Sally considered medicine but dismissed the idea because few women (30 years ago only 8 percent of medical students were women) were accepted to medical school.

Sally always believed that she would go to graduate school once her two daughters entered high school. What would she study? Although she had no formal medical training, Sally was deeply involved in her husband's practice. He discussed medicine and related medical issues with her, and as a trained artist, she often prepared his medical illustrations.

Her turning point was triggered by two unrelated events that took place in the late 1970s. At 35, Sally began seriously to consider a number of career alternatives. She found that medicine was the only field to which she could make a serious commitment.

About this time, she met a woman doctor. Sally said to her, "You're doing what I want to do, and the doctor said 'then do it'." A U.S. Supreme Court decision provided the real incentive when it ruled that the University of California had practiced reverse discrimination when it denied medical school admission to 38-year-old Alan Bakke.

Like most older applicants, she followed a prescribed series of premed courses. "Since I was anchored to the New York area by family ties and my husband's New Jersey medical practice, I applied to seven local medical schools. Like the experience faced by Margaret Spinelli, there were some subtle and some not so subtle discrimination, including one admissions officer who said that my place should be at home taking care of the family."

"When I started taking premed courses, Steve was at first cautious, but as I moved closer to admission he became excited. He acted as the family buffer, explaining to our teenage daughters what was taking place and why."

Accepted to the Columbia University Medical School–College of Physicians & Surgeons, Sally's life changed drastically. Other than spending time with Steve and the children, all social life stopped. Sally hired a housekeeper, and rather than live on campus, she commuted each day to New York City.

"It was not a bad time to be an older woman in medical school. And being married to a physician, I felt comfortable with both students and doctors."

As have many career changers, Sally appreciated the advantages of being an older student. Her sensitivity to an older patient's needs were sharpened even more when both her parents died while she was attending medical school. Nor was she a medical romantic.

"At my age, there was no peer pressure to go to medical school. I can assure you it was all voluntary. I was more fortunate than most of my classmates in other ways. I did not have to worry about finances. Unlike most of my classmates, who were single, I had to compromise on my family life, but the trade-off was worth it."

From Air Force Jets to Anesthesiology

Captain Jeffrey Croy (midthirties) was a U.S. Air Force hurricane hunter with over 2000 hours of flying time as a weather reconnaissance pilot. Jeff, in keeping with a long-term career plan, gave up a promising military career for medicine.

When he graduated from the U.S Air Force Academy, he was ninth in a class of 899 cadets. A major in biologic sciences, Jeff wanted to be a doctor. He even went so far as to take the MCATs, and he could have gone to medical school at no cost as an Air Force officer. He decided to delay medical training. He reasoned that there was a lot to be learned about people before he could be an effective doctor. Besides, Jeff always wanted to fly. His Air Force career represented only a temporary delay.

When Jeff was nearing the end of the required six-year service commitment, he applied to medical school. By then he was married and the father of two of their three children. Raised in Oregon, Jeff was not restricted geographically to any section of the country. Jeff was attracted to the University of Rochester because he liked its philosophy of social and humanistic medicine.

Once the Croys moved from Texas to Rochester, Jeff had to adjust to medical school after a seven-year absence from the classroom. Besides competing with students directly out of college, it was difficult to get back into the academic mode.

"In the Academy, memorizing was never a problem, but as a pilot I became more selective, only memorizing things of critical importance to the mission. I soon learned that this approach does not work in medical school."

In other ways, Jeff had to change some personal mannerisms. As a husband, father, and pilot, he was used to responsibility and as military officer and pilot, he assumed a leadership role, but as a medical student he realized that he needed to modify these traits.

Now the father of three children, Jeff had limited financial resources, which hardly changed over four years in Rochester. A scholarship, student loans, some savings, and frugality, along with on-campus student housing, helped offset expenses. For a brief period, his wife, Denise, worked nights as a waitress while he studied and babysat.

After graduating from Rochester in June 1991, Jeff returned to the Northwest and a four-year intern and residency program in anesthesiology at the University of Washington Hospital in Seattle. "There actually is a close correlation between anesthesiology and flying weather reconnaissance missions. In both jobs, you must adjust rapidly to change and react to emergencies. As a pilot, the critical part of each mission is the take off and landing; in medicine, it is the patient's entering into and coming out of anesthesia."

To Medical School via the Newsroom

"Going into medicine was like returning to my roots. I hardly remembered my father, who was a cardiologist. He died in an airplane crash when I was three."

Geoffrey Quinn (midthirties), now a resident in internal medicine at New York Hospital, entered Cornell Medical College in 1988. When he started at the University of California–Los Angeles in the mid-1970s, he was a premed student but soon switched to history.

The Woodward and Bernstein era of investigative reporting attracted him to journalism, and he spent the next eight years as a freelancer, newsletter editor, and reporter with Associated Press. He even took a year off to get a master degree from Columbia's Graduate School of Journalism.

Geoff, by all indications, was a career journalist. He had married Christine Weicher, a television news reporter. "Just before we left on our honeymoon, I learned that the AP wanted to transfer me from Hartford to the Miami bureau. I was unhappy about the reassignment."

Chris knew that Geoff once flirted with a medical career, so when he indicated that he was now interested in being a doctor she said he should give it a try. Her challenge was direct. If he did well in his premed courses, she'd provide the ongoing financial support while he attended medical school. Geoff was an indifferent UCLA undergraduate, but he made straight A's in his predoc courses.

They moved to California (he's from San Diego and Chris is from northern California), and Geoff worked as a laboratory assistant while Chris was assigned by CBS-TV to its local station. After applying to 19 different medical schools, he was accepted at Cornell—by far the most expensive. As a California resident, he would have qualified for free tuition.

Attending Cornell meant scaling down their standard of living. They returned to New York and rented out their Greenwich Village apartment, paid all debts, and moved into subsidized student housing adjacent to Cornell's New York campus. Except for the period when she was on pregnancy and maternity leave, Chris supported the family.

Being a medical school student did not curtail Geoff's interest in social issues. During his first year, he founded Cornell's Homeless First Aid Project, in which student volunteers provide basic first aid treatment and referrals to homeless people living in Grand Central Station.

"As a medical school applicant, some admission interviewers questioned my news background, yet I've found it a very useful medical tool. Surprisingly, there are many parallels. In journalism, you are required to meet deadlines. You learn to listen, ask good questions, and then, in a news story, accurately summarize what you've observed. A good doctor goes through a similar process by getting patients to tell their stories, asking pertinent questions, and then summarizing the diagnosis in a medical history.

"There are, however, some noticeable differences. Journalists are primarily observers but a doctor becomes a direct participant. If a journalist makes a mistake, the most that can happen is being fired or sued. When you are a doctor, the patient dies."

From Show Business to Medicine

Brendan Greer (midthirties), once a financial consultant in the entertainment industry and now a surgical resident at Temple Hospital in Philadelphia, is one of Geoff Quinn's classmates. The differences stop here, for Brendan never considered a medical career until he was in his early thirties.

Raised in Florida, where his father was an English professor, Brendan went to Harvard College, majored in medieval English literature, and then continued in a master program in the same subject at the University of Toronto. If he had any career goal at the time, it was museum management.

To increase his employment opportunities, he earned an MBA from the University of Pennsylvania Wharton School of Finance and was hired by a management consulting firm. Two years later, he joined Silver Screen Management, which forms limited partnerships to fund Hollywood films. After a few years, he became bored with the work. If he was seriously interested in furthering his career in the film business, Brendan admits that he should have moved to California and worked for a film company.

"Until I was nearly 30 I never thought of being a doctor. At Harvard, I steered clear of science courses. Silver Screen's office was on the east side of New York, and one evening after work I walked over to Cornell, the medical school nearest my office. Without an appointment, I just asked one of the admission officers how one gets into medical school. He suggested enrolling in either Columbia or the Hunter College premed program. I selected Hunter because it was a city school and had a low tuition and it was convenient to my office."

Previously an average student, Brendan's high premed grades qualified him for early admission to Cornell as a Hunter linkage student. By now, he was working part-time at Silver Screen so he could take additional premed courses and accelerate his entrance into Cornell.

His entry into medicine was a shock. He had to rely on brute memorization, a skill he had not perfected in his past schooling. Brendan, who is single, financed medical school with loans. As a former financial manager, he considered the return on investment to be excellent if he invested his savings in his professional training.

Other medical students for convenience or economy live in student housing, but Brendan, who is single, kept his apartment a few blocks from Cornell. This increased his living expenses but was consistent with his goal to maintain a separate personal life.

The Chairman of the Board in Medical School

Approaching the George Washington Bridge on the New Jersey side, drivers can hardly miss a nine-story brick office building, the headquarters for On-Line Software International's headquarters, which until its acquisition in September 1991 was a publicly owned company with sales in excess of $100 million.

On-Line Software's chairman and chief executive officer is Jack Berdy (midforties), who founded the company in 1969.

Different from nearly all other CEOs whose total time is spent running their companies, Jack took a leave of absence to attend the George Washington University School of Medicine in Washington, D.C. while continuing to serve as On-Line Software's CEO.

After graduating from a New York high school, Jack entered the University of Maryland as a premed student and a microbiology major. Two years later, he quit college for personal and financial reasons and spent several years working as a systems analyst for Sperry Rand Corporation (now Unisys Corporation) and IBM Corporation.

An entrepreneur and risk taker, he started On-Line Software when he was 22, and over the next two decades it thrived. Jack never forgot his initial career objective, however.

In the late 1980s, Jack completed his undergraduate degree at Fairleigh Dickinson University, where he is also a trustee. He found that preparing academically represented one challenge, but getting into medical school was more traumatic.

"My biggest problem was to get medical schools to take me seriously. Admission officers thought I was having a midlife crisis and, if I was accepted, I would never finish. They couldn't understand how I was going to handle both medical school and my responsibilities at On-Line Software." Their attitude changed after he completed his second year and Jack transferred from George Washington to the Mt. Sinai School of Medicine in New York, nearer both home and office.

Since the company had a structured corporate management, Jack left day-to-day operations to staff members. Even so, during the first two years in medical school in Washington he spent an hour or so each day talking with employees by telephone or electronic mail and by direct contact on weekend commutes to New Jersey.

Following his second year of medical school, On-Line Software was sold to Computer Associates International for $120 million, a purchase that gave Jack, the company's major shareholder, $23 million in cash.

Medical school, at best, is a grueling experience, which is further compounded when you're living a dual life, but Jack was used to a vigorous lifestyle and three to four hours of sleep a night. His experience building On-Line Software was actually excellent preparation for medical school. Unlike many younger students, he knew how to organize sheer volumes of materials, how to put things into order and then work on them systematically.

Jack's training as a programmer and systems analyst also proved an advantage in his combined student and executive life-style. He created a self-teaching, question-and-answer software program consisting of the 12,000 medical terms that students are required to learn during their first two years.

Although he is no longer associated with Computer Associates, Jack expects to apply his computer skills and financial resources to support a lifelong interest in immunology and clinical research.

She'll Become a Doctor When She's in Her Midfifties

By the time Julia Chase Brand (late forties) completes medical school and residency, she'll be nearly 55 years old. Julia, who joined the Barnard College faculty in 1976, was a tenured associate professor and chair of the biology department. She's no novice when it comes to medical school protocols, having been a member of Barnard's premed advisory committee.

When Julia graduated from Smith College in 1965, she enrolled in a combined MD/PhD program at Indiana University. Soon afterward, she was diagnosed as having multiple sclerosis. Although it later proved to be an incorrect diagnosis, she dropped out of the medical program but received her doctorate in physiology in the early 1970s.

The idea of becoming a doctor, however, was never forgotten. "When I was in my early thirties George (Brand) and I got married; I knew my biological clock was running and I deferred medical school to have children. John was born but I also had several miscarriages. The idea of medical school was deferred until John was older. Now that he was nearly a teenager, I was able to consider medical school. And, I felt that I had gone as far as I could go in academia."

As a Barnard premed advisor, Julia was familiar with medical school entrance requirements, and her name was also known by many admission officers. She was disappointed with medical school admission practices.

"Due to equal opportunity rulings, the real issues were never openly discussed, but a number of the admission directors asked indirect questions about my health and my ability to complete medical training when I would be 55.

Julia followed the advice that she gave her premed students: keep a sense of humor, and don't bristle when equal opportunity items are raised. Your job is to get into medical school.

Because of a number of personal obligations, made even more complex by resigning from a $40,000 tenured Barnard job, Julia was limited to medical schools near her northern New Jersey home. Like Blanche Skurnick, she entered New Jersey's state medical school, with a tuition less than one-half the rate of most other medical schools in the metropolitan New York area.

To partially pay for medical school, Julia took advantage of an available Barnard sabbatical to cover some of her first-year expenses. When her schedule permits, she teaches biology on a part-time basis.

Events from her past also influence the possible direction she might take as an older physician. As a Smith student, she was a marathon runner and tried out for several Olympic teams in the 1960s. Her father was an alcoholic, and as a result, she is considering specializing in sports medicine and alcoholism.

CAREER OPPORTUNITIES AS A NURSE

After a decade of declining enrollment, there is an upswing in nursing school enrollment. The ability to add 200,000 more nurses to the employment pool should help lessen severe anticipated shortages of professional staffs in hospitals and health care facilities. Nursing is benefiting from the economic downswing as both teenage college entrants and older career changers recognize some of the pitfalls of a business career.

THE MARKETPLACE

The American Nursing Association reports that there are an estimated 2.2 million registered nurses: 80 percent, or over 1.6 million, work in hosptials and the balance in nursing homes, doctor's offices, schools, or the government; 25 percent of registered nurses work part-time.

The health care industry needs to create approximately 350,000 registered nursing jobs during the 1990s. It would seem, based on a National League for Nursing study, that the shortage would decrease as the current 250,000 enrolled student nurses enter the profession. Unfortunately, for every 10 students, only 4 graduate, and 1 of these will fail to pass qualifying tests.

The shortage is actually expanding as experienced hospital nurses find higher paying and less demanding jobs with insurance companies, health maintenance organizations, and home care facilities.

Career switching to nursing has already changed the age of entry-level nurses: the average for new nurses is approximately 31, six to seven years older than a decade ago.

The job market, the U.S. Bureau of Labor Statistics reports, should be very good for some time. Among the factors that drive this growth are the technical advances in patient care and the larger number of older people requiring treatment.

Like a number of other professions, recruitment remains a problem in rural and some urban hospitals. Some nurses are finding entrepreneurial opportunities and higher incomes in providing home health care services.

HOW TO ENTER THE FIELD

The process starts by graduating from an approved nursing school and passing a national nursing test administered on the state level. Approximately 1460 schools offer certified nursing training in three different curricula: 488 colleges have four- to five-year degree-granting programs; 812 offer two-year associate degree programs, mostly through community colleges; and the balance, or about 157, are nursing schools affiliated with hospitals.

Tuition varies from the higher costs at private colleges to the less expensive state and community colleges. Scholarship, tuition grants, and cooperative hospital programs are available.

SOCIAL AND PROFESSIONAL OBSTACLES FACING CAREER SWITCHERS

Make no mistake about it, nursing is very demanding physically. The hours are long. Hospitals and other primary care health care facilities operate on a 24-hour day. Hospital duty and its life-saving responsibilities place additional pressures on nurses.

THE WOMEN'S ISSUE

Even with some nursing schools actively trying to recruit male nurses, men comprise less than 5 percent of the registered nurses, a figure that has not changed significantly in 20 years. At the end of the Vietnam War, returning veterans used health care skills learned in the service and became nurses. Early retiree police and firefighters from time to time enter nursing.

Even with what appear to be statistics that highly favor women, there is an imbalance. Over 95 percent of registered nurses are women, but the breakdown, according to a Case Western Reserve University study, differs sharply among nurse anesthetists. In a specialty in which salaries start at $70,000, the ratios change: only 55 percent of the nation's 25,000 certified anesthetists are women.

THE PAY

The starting salaries nationally are approximately $25,000, but in some larger metropolitan centers beginners earn up to $35,000. Entry-level salaries are lower in the South and Southwest and higher in the Northeast and California. Experienced nurses average $32,000, with heads of hospital nursing departments earning about $42,000.

THE CAREER SWITCHERS

An Executive Secretary Turns to Nursing

If a close friend hadn't died of lung cancer in November 1988, chances are Marilyn Owens (late thirties) would still be working as executive secretary to the chief financial officer of CPC International, the producers of Skippy peanut butter, Hellmann's mayonnaise, and Thomas' English muffins. Instead Marilyn is a nurse, earning about $30,000 a year.

"When my friend was diagnosed as having terminal cancer, I helped take care of him until he died. This experience started me thinking that there must be more to life than what I was doing." For 12 years, Marilyn had a secure job at the same company, several weeks of vacation, benefits for herself and two teenage daughters, and regular salary increases.

"On New Year's Eve, as is the custom in our family, I stayed at home with my two daughters. I used the evening to reflect on the past year and to look ahead. As much as I liked my work, I didn't want to be doing the same thing for another 20 years. I thought about my friend. Perhaps it was his illness and death that brought me to nursing."

Marilyn, limited by finances and family responsibilities to a nursing school in northern New Jersey, considered both two- and four-year programs. She took a required basic chemistry course and was accepted to Englewood Hospital's two-year certification program, less than a mile from home.

When she told her boss that she was leaving CPC, he was actually relieved. He thought the time that Marilyn was taking off, which was inconsistent with her usual work habits, meant that she was looking for another job. Nursing school proved to be a humbling educational experience. After a 19-year absence from school, she had difficulty with her studies. Marilyn's work experience was helpful in her clinical assignments, however. She understood the practical politics of business, the chain of command, and how to deal effectively with different types of personalities.

First an Accountant, Then a Nurse

Jerry Green's (late thirties) corporate job in Oregon was eliminated by a computerized financial system. One day he was a middle manager with his own support staff; the next day he was drawing barely enough unemployment compensation to meet monthly mortgage payments.

While scanning the classifieds, he found only 16 ads for accountants, compared with three pages of ads for nurses. When Jerry announced he was planning to enter nursing school, friends and relatives questioned his decision. In an article in the *American Journal of Nursing,* Jerry noted that "my nine year old son couldn't believe his ears. 'Aren't nurses mommies?' he asked. His question reflected more than its apparent sexist overtones. In our family, the mommy is a nurse, and the daddy is (or was) an accountant."

From Volunteer to Nurse

When Ruth Adelman (late forties) left her Philadelphia home nearly 30 years ago to attend Barnard College, her father, a university law professor, advised her not to be a nurse.

Like so many women college students a generation ago, Ruth married during her senior year. At the time, a college degree was cynically described as an "Mrs." She then worked for the New York City Board of Education in its planning department, moved to New Jersey, had two sons, and became involved in family counseling and as a hospice volunteer.

Little did she realize hospice work was the catalyst to a new career. "My work with terminally ill patients helped me to mature. I was spending about 10 hours a week as a volunteer, and I became interested in nursing as I watched nurses attend terminally ill patients. I got hooked, but I could just as easily have become a social worker. But nursing offered a medical involvement. I started to investigate and learned there was an acute shortage of nurses."

Her husband, Phil, was then in the early stages of a career change (see Phil Adelman in Chapter 11). Ruth spent a year taking college-level preparation courses in science to qualify for the Columbia School of Nursing two-year program for students who already had a bachelor's degree.

There was an advantage in being an older nursing student. Like other career changers in the health care field, Ruth found that younger students had more difficulty coping with life-and-death situations. She was also a straight A student, an improvement over her average Barnard grades.

Following graduation, Ruth worked for several years as a nurse at an adult day-care center. As her next challenge, she received a master degree in psychiatric nursing, the credentials needed in her present work in geriatric psychotherapy.

Points to Remember

- ▶ Not everyone thinks career changers should become physicians.
- ▶ There is a trend toward more age 35 plus medical students.
- ▶ A predoc program is important.
- ▶ Midlife career changers are encouraged to train as primary health care physicians.
- ▶ Age is sometimes a deterring factor in getting into medical school.
- ▶ Medical school is an academic as well as a physical grind.
- ▶ The gender issue persists.
- ▶ The nursing shortage continues.
- ▶ Career changers are welcome in nursing.
- ▶ Even in nursing, there is a gender problem.

CHAPTER 11

Law

CAREER OPPORTUNITIES

The legal profession has long been a revolving door, with lawyers exiting for careers in business, government, and other professions (a number are profiled in *It's Never Too Late*).

The difference today is that the departure rate appears to be accelerating. Surveys conducted by no less an authority than the American Bar Association confirm the growing level of dissatisfaction within the profession.

In *Running from the Law*, lawyer and author Deborah Arron noted that an estimated 5 percent, or 30,000 of the nation's lawyers, are actively considering other careers.

The reasons for leaving vary. A survey conducted by *California Lawyer* indicates that only 9 percent of lawyers are totally satisfied with their careers and 70 percent, if they had the opportunity, would start a new career. Even with what appears a disgruntled profession, upward of 9 percent of law school entrants are over 35. Each dropout seems to be replaced by an older career changer.

In my talks with lawyers who have switched to other fields, a few indicated that they were never fully committed to a legal career even when they attended law school. Legal training was intended as a professional basis for a career in business, corporate management, or government service. This is not surprising. Legal training has long been considered a stepping-stone and entrée into careers other than law.

The American Bar Association finds that 30 percent of all lawyers admitted to practice law actually work in a nonrelated field. The exceptions are corporate lawyers, who are still considered practicing attorneys.

The legal profession is changing. Gone is the clubby and at times loosely structured work environment of a generation ago. Midsized to large law firms mirror what is taking place throughout the corporate world: they're merging, being acquired, reducing staffs, and, in some instances, even going out of business.

Also vanishing is the traditional concept of lifelong tenure for law firm partners. Unheard of a generation ago, law firms are terminating employment contracts with partners and senior support personnel.

Another trend seems to have accelerated in recent years. Nonpracticing lawyers regard legal training as on a par with getting an MBA. For them, the law was never a "calling" but rather a skill to be used in conjunction with other occupations—real estate, investment banking, or business.

As lawyers exit from full-time practice, they create opportunities for career changers. This game of musical chairs fortunately has some advantages. It creates job openings that can be filled by career switchers, who often bring with them talents and experience from other fields.

THE MARKETPLACE

The ABA estimates that there are approximately 780,000 practicing lawyers. On average, over the past few years about 74 percent are employed in solo or group practices, 13 percent work for the government or as judges, 12 percent as internal counsel in corporate and nonprofit organizations, and 1 percent in legal education.

The number of lawyers admitted annually to the bar has more than tripled in less than 25 years, from 14,644 new lawyers in 1967 to 47,147 in 1990. Besides the traditional sources of employment, lawyers are also finding jobs in consumer and environmental protection and civil rights advocacy, legal disciplines literally unknown 25 years ago.

Since there are no age restrictions to practicing law, becoming a lawyer at 50 poses few problems. Unlike the corporate world, with its enforced retirement, a lawyer is an unfettered, free agent. A judge, house counsel, or law firm partner might retire to take advantage of a pension, yet the same lawyer is free to practice indefinitely. This factor encourages midcareer changers to make the switch.

The career switcher brings certain advantages to the law: the actor turned lawyer is doubly qualified as an entertainment lawyer or the former social worker often has a decided advantage in divorce or family practice law.

Lawyers, the U.S. Bureau of Labor Statistics reports, will continue to encounter competitive employment conditions through the year 2005. The number of graduating lawyers remains at a level at which they cannot all be fully absorbed into the economy. The best employment opportunities are in salaried corporate and government jobs as staff attorneys or with midsized to large firms.

Law school graduates with high class rankings have the best chance for jobs with the larger national and regional law firms. Establishing a new practice should be easiest in small communities and expanding suburban areas.

HOW TO ENTER THE FIELD

Few shortcuts exist in applying and then attending law school and in being admitted to the bar. The 175 American Bar Association-approved law schools are located in every state except Alaska, Nevada, Rhode Island, and the Commonwealth of Puerto Rico. Unlike medical schools, which require a mandatory sequence of science courses to qualify for entry, law schools have few prerequisite academic requirements.

Law schools seek applicants with rich and diverse experiences; astronomy and zoology majors are as welcome as political scientists. Nearly all ABA-approved schools require applicants to take the Law School Aptitude Tests, a standardized measurement of reading comprehension and analytic and logical reasoning, capabilities considered essential to law school success.

Since LSAT scores influence admission decisions, applicants should prepare for these tests either by taking cram courses or by using self-help books and audiovisual training aids. This is especially important to midlife career changers, whose academic training might have been completed 10, 20, or more years ago.

In addition to the ABA-accredited schools, another 40 law schools (27 in California) operate without ABA sanction, says *Barron's Guide to Law Schools.* Beware the pitfalls in attending a nonaccredited school (not that they bilk their students or fail to provide a decent legal education). Rather, nonaccredited schools limit possible job and career opportunities. Because they fail to meet the ABA academic guidelines, it is nearly impossible for a graduate to take a bar examination outside the state in which the school is located. Why attend a nonaccredited school and realize these pitfalls? These schools tend to attract students who might normally not qualify for admission to an accredited school.

A further note of caution: career changers should be aware that proportionally fewer graduates of nonaccredited schools pass state bar examinations than graduates of accredited institutions. This problem does not overly concern them. Their objective is to practice law in California or to use their legal training as the basis for a career in business or some other field.

To the joy of career changers, law schools know their demographics and the markets they serve: 79 of the 175 approved law schools operate evening divisions and offer programs requiring four rather than the usual three years of study. These schools are nearly all located in major downtown and suburban hubs, and other than their late afternoon and evening class schedules, the curriculum and support services are identical to those in the day division.

Some law schools, however, frown upon an evening school education. Despite their objection that evening school represents an academic and professional compromise, evening school nonetheless complements the realistic work and study needs of many career changers.

There is a distinct difference among national, state, and local law schools, a differential that is minimal in terms of a quality education. Harvard, Duke, or Stanford University graduates, more often than not, seek jobs outside the law school's immediate geographic jurisdiction—thus their classification as national law schools.

Graduates of the state law schools, normally part of the state university system, tend to practice law in the state or the general region; graduates of local law schools find employment in closer proximity to the law school.

Tuition is on a par with that for other graduate school programs. National law schools, which are nearly all privately owned, cost more than state-supported and local schools. Evening schools provide career changers with an opportunity to work while they study and, in some instances, to qualify for corporate reimbursement plans. Student loans, fellowships, and scholarships are available to both day and evening division law students.

SOCIAL AND PROFESSIONAL OBSTACLES FACING CAREER SWITCHERS

You're on your own in finding a job. In a healthy economic period, the top students, usually law review editors, have little difficulty attracting the attention of the major law firms and the judiciary. Even here the recession has taken its toll. A number of large firms have reduced their on-campus recruitment. Career switchers, however, face a different set of challenges.

The 35-plus graduate should look at age as an asset. Don't underplay the advantages of being a trained engineer, teacher, or city planner. These credentials are door openers to employment with niche specialty law firms and corporate law departments.

Most lawyers practice in the major metropolitan centers. The American Bar Association finds that approximately 48 percent of lawyers practice alone, contradicting what sometimes appears to be a profession dominated by large firms.

Career switchers generally find it more difficult to find entry-level jobs in the larger law firms. When they do, the 45-year-old career changer should not expect to become a partner. There are exceptions, but as a rule these firms employ younger lawyers who can make a greater economic and longer professional contribution. If partnership is a professional goal, the opportunities exist with small to midsized general practice and niche or specialty firms.

Finding a job is a marketing challenge. The process starts with a resumé that needs to read differently than those prepared by younger lawyers. Even though law school placement specialists advise graduates to prepare a resumé that plays down milestone dates—year of college graduation, military service, and other data that underscore age—it can be assumed that questions related to age will be asked during job interviews.

Placement specialists recommend that job applicants stress their dual skills. An engineer applying for a job with a patent law firm or as house counsel for an electronics company has an advantage.

The job interview establishes other potential obstacles. Avoid talking about children, and definitely not grandchildren, or referring to events that took place 25 years ago as though they were only yesterday. Appearing in a mother or father role model, although socially appealing, tends to undermine the perceived ability to function as an older professional who may be reporting to a much younger supervisor.

THE WOMEN'S ISSUE

Differing little from the demographics in other occupations, men dominate the upper echelons of nearly all major law firms and judgeships, as well as the legal departments in industry and government. Statistics on law school admissions signal future employment opportunities for women. In the mid-1960s, 4 percent of the law school students were women; 25 years later, it is nearing parity.

THE PAY

Other than firms with over 250 lawyers in which new attorneys are paid approximately $70,000, the national average for 1990 graduates was $50,960. In its most recent employment and salary survey, the National Association of Law Placement noted that a salary differential exists among legal specialties.

Corporate lawyers start at $46,260. Judicial clerks, considered one of the most prestigious entry-level jobs, are paid $28,740, slightly less than the salaries for new government lawyers, who earn $31,000. It is hardly a surprise that public interest lawyers earn the least, at $27,070, and those teaching law are paid $37,400. Newly employed lawyers in California receive $54,000, compared with $48,000 in Texas and $24,500 in Iowa.

THE CAREER SWITCHERS

Amusement Park Operator Practices Corporate Law

In 1941, when Norman Tanenbaum (midsixties) was 16, he was a freshman studying mechanical engineering at the University of Missouri. Too young at the time for military service, he went into the merchant marine as an engineering officer when he graduated three years later.

Following three years of service, Norman found and soon lost a job with a government contractor as an engineer. Unemployment taught him an important lesson: the need for a more secure profession or business. Even so, he drifted until his midthirties into a series of different businesses before making a midlife commitment.

His entrepreneurial career started when he developed Uncle Milton's Amusement Park, actually named after his partner and brother but meant to cash in on the popularity of the comedian and TV star of the period, Milton Berle. Although financially successful, the park after several seasons had reached its maximum size. Norman, now in his early thirties, was no longer challenged. He drifted again.

Responding to the booming post-World War II real estate market, Norman built and sold low-cost homes. He sold over 100 homes his first year but his marketing formula was copied by other local builders.

With income from the sale of the amusement park and from a daytime real estate job, Norman entered the New York University School of Law, graduating first in the evening division and as a law review editor. He was unsure of his professional goals.

"I naively turned down a possible offer to become law clerk to the chief justice of the California courts. I didn't want to move my wife and three children to California. I never realized that a clerkship would lead to job offers. As an entrepreneur, I knew I didn't have the temperament to join a large law firm with the hopes of someday becoming a partner. I wanted more rapid promotion and quicker professional and financial recognition. Instead, I went to work for a small New York City firm and in two years became a partner."

Norman was then hired by a real estate company as its house counsel. A few years later, he joined his current firm and became a partner. Nearly 50 years after graduating from college as a mechanical engineer, he continues to use his earlier training. Engineering, real estate, business, and the law all relate. Each has a bearing on the others. One client developed a heat exchanger, and from his merchant marine experience, he understands how a power plant works. These skills acquired over a lifetime enable him to serve his clients better.

From Sausage Maker to Lawyer

James Chase (early fifties) has all the earmarks of a high achiever. As a result of a number of interrelating personal problems, Jim didn't start to put his own house in order until he was in his midthirties.

After flunking out of Hamilton College after the second semester, Jim held a series of lower level bank and financial service company jobs, nearly all below his natural potential. In 1974, Jim was hired as office manager by a New Haven, Connecticut sausage maker, a small family-owned company with 100 employees. He soon became the unofficial second in command. By this time, he was in an alcoholic recovery program and had received a bachelor degree with highest honors from Quinnipiac

College, winning the college's outstanding evening student award in his junior year.

Although he had a secure job at the sausage company, he was 41 and still a generalist. There was little future for him other than working for smaller companies as a financial manager. The law would perhaps provide the professional credentials he wanted. While attending Quinnipiac, Jim took the law boards, placed in the top 1 percent nationally, and entered the University of Connecticut Law School in Hartford. Over the next four years, he attended law school at night and drove nearly 80 miles round-trip several nights a week.

Jim graduated with honors and several academic awards. His boss had little idea that he was living a dual life. "When I graduated and I passed the bar, I was still working for the sausage company. My boss's wife saw my name in the newspaper. She called my wife and asked if the 'Jim Chase' was the same person who worked for her husband. My wife answered that it was just another of my hobbies—attending law school."

After working three years for a Bridgeport law firm, Jim became a public defender in New Haven. In his second year on the job, he handled over 800 cases, only 2 ever coming to trial.

"My life has finally come together. As a public defender, I like the idea of not having to look for clients." His past personal problems enable him to deal effectively with his clients, 50 percent of whom have some form of addiction. "I feel good about myself. When I had troubles, others came to my help. Now I'm in the position to repay."

The Political Scientist Turns to Law

After more than 15 years of teaching political science at several New York area colleges and working as an independent public administration consultant, Sara Silbiger's (early fifties) lawyer husband challenged her. "Why not be a lawyer? The law is a far better index of judging your intellectual capabilities than teaching or consulting." Sara was then 43, and she took his challenge seriously.

Sara had never considered law as a career when she graduated from Barnard College in 1960. Her father and other family members were lawyers, but law school for most women was not a professional option. At the time, there were only 10 women in a class of several hundred law students at Harvard University. Like many women of that generation, she became a teacher, got married, and had children. Yet unlike most women of that generation, she received a doctorate in political science and public administration from New York University. This provided the academic basis to teach government at the university level and to serve as a consultant on labor and political issues.

In the early 1980s, Sara considered career alternatives, seeking one that would synthesize a number of her skills. "As in most things in my life, I do not operate with a long-term plan. I just let things happen and, if I became a lawyer, it would be a distinct profession, not an extension of teaching or additional background for labor law." She took a cram course to prepare for the law boards with the intention to apply to law school if she did well.

Family commitments limited her geographically to a few law schools in New York City. She selected the Fordham University School of Law, where the dean's list and the law review led to an appointment as a student clerk to a Federal District Court magistrate and a summer clerkship at Debevoise & Plimpton, one of the larger New York law firms. Following graduation in 1986, she was hired as an associate by the firm. In the first year on the job, she tripled her previous combined earnings as a teacher and consultant.

Now as an associate with over six years of corporate and litigation experience, Sara intends to remain with her firm as a senior associate for the immediate future.

She enjoys the intellectual demands of an aggressive corporate law firm, but Sara anticipates that age and an accompanying reluctance to make the personal sacrifices required of newer and potential partners will dictate a need to rethink her legal career goals within the next few yers.

From Advertising to White-Collar Crime Litigator

For nearly 20 years, Charles David Kreps, Jr. (late forties) succeeded in what Benjamin Disraeli in another era described as the climb "to the top of the greasy pole." Akin to Disraeli's late nineteenth century rise to parliamentary power, David prospered professionally and financially in the highly competitive New York advertising agency business.

In a series of jobs representing the normal advertising agency employment pattern, David rose to vice president, management supervisor, and package goods specialist at one of the nation's top 10 agencies, supervising British Airways, Campbell Soup Company, Frito-Lay, Inc. and Sears Roebuck and Company. During this time, he took two brief leaves of absence to serve as special assistant to New York Senator James L. Buckley.

"Starting in the early 1980s, I found that an advertising agency was no longer a 'fun place' to work as bottom-line orientation got the best of agency operations. In considering career alternatives, I knew that the law was the only thing, other than advertising, that I ever thought about doing."

David entered the Fordham School of Law Evening Division in 1983, coincidental with a period when he was changing jobs more frequently than usual. One employer showed little respect for his legal studies, and another was actually hostile, viewing it as a professional conflict of interest. When he lost his last agency job as a result of a management shake-up, David took a less pressured, nine to five job as marketing director of an insurance brokerage firm, a position that enabled him to concentrate on law school studies.

If David was interested in legal work related to advertising, his past marketing experience might have been an employment asset. Instead he selected litigation and criminal law and was hired by a firm specializing in tax and white-collar crime. Even in this unrelated field, there are carryover benefits from his advertising career.

"Unlike most other new lawyers, I already knew how to work with clients. After more than four years, I'm making about $70,000 a year, somewhat less than my last agency job, but like advertising was 15 years ago, it's a fun place to work."

From a Family Business to Law School

"At the same time as my wife, Ruth, started nursing school in 1983, I sold my business. While I was sorting out future plans, I also had more time to spend with my sons."

Philip Adelman (late forties), like several others in this book, is only one-half of a career-switching husband-and-wife team (see Ruth Adelman's profile in Chaper 10). When Phil was 42, he sold Adelman Stationery Company, an office equipment firm, which he took over in 1970 when its owner, his uncle, became ill. During his 13-year tenure, Phil ugraded the business, adding new features that included computers and a catalog operation. He ran the company by applying the know-how learned earlier in his career as a marketing manager for CPC International and as a Columbia University MBA student.

"I changed Adelman Stationery from a mom-and-pop business. Sales quadrupled. Our second store was producing sales of

$400,000 a year and was highly profitable. We had 22 full- and part-time employees. Since I never liked the routine job of running the business, I hired a general manager and I concentrated on expanding the business." It was an excellent relationship, which ended abruptly seven years later when he was hit by a truck and could no longer work. His replacement didn't work out. "I once again became involved in day-to-day operations. I got itchy to make a permanent change."

Phil's initial intention after selling Adelman Stationery was to earn a doctorate in management and teach college. Looking realistically at the college job market, he was unwilling to spend the time only to face the uncertainties of finding a job.

As an alternative, Phil sold industrial real estate and became a fundraiser for a nonprofit organization. "For the first time in my life, I was at loose ends. Up to the time I decided to study for the law boards, the idea of being a lawyer was a fantasy."

A New Jersey resident, Phil applied to the state's only two law schools, at Seton Hall and Rutgers universities, since the cost was one-half the tuition of the New York City law schools. Until he entered law school, Phil had little idea how, if at all, his business experience would prove helpful. Trained initially in market research, he learned that there is a close correlation between the question-and-answer techniques used in market research and legal questioning.

Living a Lifelong Dream

Susan Rolon (midthirties) lives an extremely busy life. Each workday, she wakes up at 6:15, walks her eight-year-old son to school, works as a curriculum supervisor at an experimental elementary school in the Bronx, and at the end of the school day takes an 8-mile subway ride to the Fordham School of Law midtown New York campus. Following class, she returns to the Bronx, eats dinner prepared by her mother, chats with her teenage daughter, studies until one, and then goes to bed.

Susan, who married after completing a year of college, moved to Virginia, where her husband was stationed in the Marine Corps. She returned to New York after her divorce and finished college. Although she took the law boards in her senior year, her first priority as a single mother was a full-time salaried job. Teaching was an important milestone in her family. A first-generation American, Susan is also the first family member to attend college.

Over the next several years, she received a master degree in reading disability and elementary education and was already being groomed as a future administrator, starting with assignments as a summer school principal.

"I enjoy teaching, but the work was becoming too routine. I was starting to lose the challenge, and I could see few long-term opportunities in education unless I moved into administration. This meant getting a doctorate."

For an equivalent investment in time and money, she preferred to go to law school. Unlike her master degree, which was paid for by the board of education, Susan is financing Fordham's four-year evening law program with a scholarship, student loans, and savings. Her daily work and study burden is lightened to some extent by her mother, who moves into her home on a Monday through Friday basis as cook, housekeeper, and sitter.

A hectic schedule has its benefits, however. She's become very well organized, applying the methodology of managing a home and classroom to her law studies. During her first year at Fordham, with the approval of her principal, she organized classroom lesson plans for the entire year in advance.

Susan expects to specialize in family practice and in legal advocacy for children. Her experience as a classroom teacher has further carryover benefits. She knows the problems firsthand when it comes to child abuse. Susan has testified before the district attorney when children in her class have been beaten or have been found with drugs.

Leaves A Family Business for Social Advocacy Law

If Leah Richter (late fifties) had been born 20 years later, she would have gone to medical school. She majored in physiology and minored in chemistry. Medicine was ruled out because of lack of money.

Instead she became a research assistant in physiology at Columbia, and as a university employee, she was entitled to take courses at no charge. In keeping with the occupational tendency for women of the era, she attended Teacher's College, where she earned a master degree in science education and then taught junior high school science.

Then (and now) Leah was interested in social issues. During the early 1960s, she was involved in the first teacher's strike in New York City's history. Leah was married and over the next few years had two sons. Again differing from many women of her generation, having children did not mean the end of her career.

"I was not the type who could keep busy as a volunteer worker. I needed more activity and tangible work. My husband had just started a dental laboratory, and I went to work with him. I ran the office and Norbert handled the technical work."

The husband-wife partnership prospered, employing 17 full-time employees who service dentists throughout the Northeast. Even with her success in business, Leah was not completely happy with the direction her career had taken. "I used to ask myself, if I'm successful at this, imagine what I could do if I really loved my work?

"I considered law my first alternative. Medicine now seemed impractical. As a lawyer, I thought I could make a difference. Going back to my teaching days, I've always been interested in the rights of children. I delayed making a decision. I had excuses. First the boys were growing up and I was needed at home; then the business was undergoing change and I couldn't walk away from my responsibilities. In my midfifties, it was either now or never."

In August 1989, Leah took the law boards after a cram course. She left the family business, and in January 1990 she entered the Benjamin N. Cardoza School of Law in New York City. The first year was exhausting. She worked 14 hours a day, six days a week commuting from New Jersey to law school, attending class, and studying. "It was hard on Norbert. Our sons were grown and living on their own. Norbert assumed the responsibility for running our home."

When Leah graduates in 1993, she plans to specialize in social advocacy law and women's issues. Like many other older career switchers, she is not relying on selling herself by resumé. Instead, she's developing related skills that will make her a more valuable lawyer. Leah works as a volunteer assistant in the law school's legal services office and clerks during the summer for a New Jersey family court judge. Leah finds the advantages of "not being afraid to roll up my sleeves" carried forward in her legal training.

———————◆———————

Points to Remember

► Career changers replace other lawyers who are exiting the profession.

► Age is not an issue in getting into law school.

► Prepare for the Law School Aptitude Tests, an important criterion for law school admission.

► In many communities, you can attend law school as a day or evening student.

► Beware of nonaccredited law schools.

► Past careers and dual skills often help get good jobs.

► Larger law firms normally shy away from employing older career changers.

———————◆———————

Clergy

CAREER OPPORTUNITIES

Think twice before a career switch to the clergy. Make no mistake about it, the clergy's life has its downside: long hours, low pay, career (particularly for the Protestant clergy), personal, and professional pressures, and, more often than not, a peripatetic lifestyle.

What's more, to climb the clerical ladder requires the multiple skills of a teacher, politician, orator, business manager, community activist, and public relations expert.

The fundamental attraction to the clergy is, of course, the spiritual involvement, followed by an opportunity, if not expected obligation, to provide active social and community leadership.

THE MARKETPLACE

Membership in the nation's Protestant churches remains comparatively static on a year-to-year basis. *The Yearbook of American and Canadian Churches* estimates that 80 million American Protestants attend church. The fundamentalist sects are growing dramatically, but there is little or no growth within the traditional Episcopal, Baptist, Methodist, and Presbyterian denominations.

The Roman Catholic Church gained in worshipers, to 57 million members, benefiting to some extent from Latin American and Caribbean immigration.

The Conservative movement has the largest number of members among the nation's nearly six million Reform, Conservative, and Orthodox Jews.

There are approximately 429,000 Protestant ministers, 52,000 Roman Catholic priests, and 7000 rabbis. Besides assignment to churches and synagogues, the balance of the ordained clergy teach, work as chaplains in the armed forces, hospitals, and prisons, or hold administrative positions with religious organizations.

Other than the fundamentalists, the job market for the Protestant clergy will stay depressed through the year 2000. In practical terms, this means that some churches are operating with smaller staffs, merging and, in a growing number of instances, even closing. The U.S. Bureau of Labor Statistics finds that a surplus of qualified Protestant ministers along with a slow growth in church membership has dampened the immediate job market.

The Roman Catholic Church faces other dilemmas. As membership rises, a shortfall exists in seminary recruitment. In some areas, the church can barely fill parish openings resulting from resignation, retirement and death. This disparity is expected to continue as long as the church upholds its historical position on celibacy and its ban on women priests.

The job market for rabbis is generally more favorable. Besides Judaism's traditional urban stronghold, new congregations are being established in smaller cities and in once religiously restricted suburban communities. Employment opportunities are also enhanced by the anticipated retirement of a large number of rabbis.

Midcareer entrants are welcome in all denominations. Age normally presents few if any barriers to seminary admission or finding a job. In the Jewish seminaries, there are proportionally fewer career switchers, compared with some Protestant seminaries, in which upward of 40 to 50 percent of the students are in their mid-thirties or older.

Previous business or professional training aside, career changers by virtue of their age have inherently acquired skills useful in the clergy: how to deal with illness, death, marriage, children, and household budgeting. These are lessons that rarely can be taught in a classroom.

This is not to say that the clergy and their congregants universally favor career changers entering the ministry. They find that they tote their own set of baggage. Career switchers are often more rigid and less adventuresome, have more personal and financial obligations, have difficulty adjusting to entry-level positions that call for "grunt" work, or are uncomfortable working for a younger boss.

HOW TO ENTER THE FIELD

There are few shortcuts to ordination, even though some fundamentalist Protestant sects prefer on-the-job training to a seminary education. Protestant, Roman Catholic, and Jewish seminaries require three to six years of seminary study before ordination. The curriculum in most instances is conducted at the graduate school level.

Before applying for admission, it is expected that applicants, regardless of age, meet and consult with the spiritual leader of the congregation where they worship. To weed out dilettantes and romantics, some seminaries even ask career switchers to take psychological tests to determine the depth of involvement.

The application process differs from seminary to seminary and from religion to religion. Like most graduate study, the first step is to review seminary catalogs. Some seminaries require the Graduate Record Examinations and completion of prerequisite courses in philosophy, religion, and foreign languages.

Latin is still the official language of the Roman Catholic Church, but fluency in Spanish is considered even more practical for priests preparing to serve in the Southwest and in many urban centers. The Jewish seminaries expect fluency in Hebrew in the very early stages of rabbinical training.

Of the approximately 200 accredited Protestant seminaries, some have national reputations and a diverse student body; others are more regional in character.

There are about 230 Roman Catholic seminaries. Entry-level requirements differ, but nearly all seminaries require applicants to have a balanced liberal arts education before admission to the four-year graduate-level curriculum.

Approximately 35 seminaries train and ordain Orthodox rabbis. The Jewish Theological Seminary of America, located in New York City, is the only seminary educating Conservative rabbis. Like the Conservatives, there is only one Reform seminary, but it maintains separate campuses in New York, Cincinnati, and Los Angeles. The typical course of study for Conservative and Reform rabbis is four to six years. The length of curriculum varies at the Orthodox seminaries.

Seminary costs are on a par with those of most graduate schools. Scholarships and grants are available. Some seminaries provide subsidized housing for married students and, to offset expenses, reluctantly permit seminarians to work part-time on holidays and vacations in non–church-related jobs.

Upon ordination, ministers are assigned to larger parishes as curates and assistant ministers or, in some instances, as ministers in small churches. Placement, however, differs among denominations.

As a hierarchic religion, the Episcopals, like the Roman Catholics, assign priests on the basis of need within the diocese. Among the less structured denominations (a similar approach applies to rabbis), the minister is a free agent, seeking employment through centralized placement offices or by networking.

The usual length of a newly ordained minister's or rabbi's first assignment is three to five years. What takes place in the clergy's employment market resembles the trend in other professions. It is easier to find employment in a rural or small town church, but most new clergy prefer jobs as assistants with larger urban or suburban churches. This provides the credentials important to professional advancement.

SOCIAL AND PROFESSIONAL OBSTACLES FACING CAREER SWITCHERS

Protestant seminarians often graduate with upward of $20,000 in debt. The prospects of a fast payback are limited by low salaries. For Protestants, there is a generally stagnant employment market and a noticeably high divorce rate. Rabbis face relatively few social problems. A major obstacle problem confronting Roman Catholic priests is the church's position on celibacy and marriage.

THE WOMEN'S ISSUE

The Protestant, Reform, and Conservative Jewish clergy continue to be male dominated. Women are still not ordained as Roman Catholic priests or as Orthodox rabbis, and even among those denominations that ordain women, career opportunities are limited. The current statistics tell a different story. Women represent a growing minority at many Protestant and Jewish seminaries, a far cry from the early 1970s, when women were refused admission by nearly all denominations. Of the 771 rabbis ordained by the Union College–Jewish Institute of Religion since 1972, more than 200 have been women.

Reporting on employment opportunities in the Jewish religion (the findings are just as applicable to most Protestant denominations), the *American Jewish Yearbook* noted that "most Reform congregations continue to express a preference for a male primary rabbi. Now that earlier female reform rabbis have attained some seniority within the movement, it remains to be seen if they will also attain rabbinical posts with the prestige and salaries commensurate with the status."

"Barbara Miller" (not her real name) became a minister in the late 1970s after a 15-year career as a classroom teacher. When Barbara (early fifties) was ordained, she turned down appointments as a hospital or college chaplain. These were safe havens for a woman minister, but she believed they represent a sellout no different from being denied a high-visibility job in corporate sales and marketing and being placed instead in a slower track corporate position.

No different from her male fellow seminarians, Barbara expected to start her career by first apprenticing for a few years as an associate pastor and then becoming pastor of her own church. This aspect of community service attracted her to the ministry. Eight years later, Barbara is still an associate pastor and past the age at which she believes she'll ever satisfy her career objective.

THE PAY

Newly ordained Protestant ministers earn, at best, in the low $20,000, and the salary level doesn't improve significantly with seniority. As partial compensation, they receive health care and retirement benefits along with possible church housing and car allowances.

The prevalent concept that the church receives two workers for the price of one has vanished; no longer does the minister's wife serve as an unpaid yet full-time assistant. This is a luxury that few male or female ministers can afford, especially those assigned to churches in wealthier urban and suburban communities. As in most professional families today, the second income is almost axiomatic.

Roman Catholic diocesan priests earn from $6000 to $10,000 annually; religious priests, who take a vow of poverty, receive no direct salaries and are supported entirely by their orders. Depending on the diocese, some diocesan priests may own and maintain property and private investments.

There was a flurry during the 1980s to adjust rabbinical salaries. Fringe benefits included, newly ordained rabbis earn between $40,000 and $60,000 or more a year. The Jewish Theological Seminary indicates salary packages of $100,000 are common for senior Reform and Conservative rabbis, and some earn twice this amount.

THE CAREER SWITCHERS

Comments from a Former Beautician

Margie Nutter (midforties), a recently ordained Lutheran minister, is a late bloomer. To Margie and her family, changing careers was a wrenching experience. It meant a change in lifestyle to achieve her goal to become a minister.

In the early 1980s, the movie, *Steel Magnolias*, could have been filmed at Margie's Hair Styling. Rather than the South, this beauty shop was located in Margie Nutter's home in Ham Lake, Minnesota, about 30 miles north of Minneapolis.

Margie, then 36, admits she never really liked doing hair, her only occupation for over 15 years, but it was a means to an end. "It gave me a chance to work at home, be available for my husband, Mike, a computer specialist with Unisys Corporation, and three children and still be active in a number of community organizations."

Her restlessness started in 1981 when she coauthored a poetry and photography book with Cheryl Meyer, one of her beauty shop's customers. She started to realize that there must be something more to life than running a beauty parlor, but it was her only source of income. "Margie's Hair Styling actually sharpened my skills. It gave me an ability to listen to people, understand their needs, and try to help them. Isn't this what the ministry is all about?"

Without a college degree, what were the alternatives? It took another three years to formulate a plan that would lead to her becoming an ordained minister. In the mid-1980s as her oldest son was entering college, she started to commute on a daily basis to Oxford College in Minneapolis. She completed a four-year undergraduate program in three and graduated summa cum laude.

In June 1992, Margie completed the four-year program at Lutheran Northwestern Theology Seminary in St. Paul and was named associate pastor of a suburban Minneapolis church.

"Going to college and seminary wasn't easy. Our marriage nearly fell apart. Since my business was at home, the family was used to having me around the house. I was no longer 'available.' We ate fast-food meals. Family life changed. Of the three children, Susan the youngest, found it the most difficult to adjust to my absence and new lifestyle. But I was determined. Now we've gotten to the point where we joke about it. My kids call me 'Pastor Mom'."

Complicating matters even further, Margie was raised a Roman Catholic and her husband was a Baptist. Earlier in their marriage, they had joined the Lutheran Church.

Reflecting on being a beautician, Margie said the job built skills useful in church work. She enjoyed working with people. Her friendships extended beyond the beauty shop. Being raised as a Catholic also had its advantages. "I spent my third year at the seminary as an intern at a midsized church in which one-third of the 800 families were former Catholics. Considering my background, I understand their needs."

Margie must have a "pied piper" personality. Her friend, Cheryl, once a school teacher, is now a professional photographer, and one of her sisters left nursing for computer programming. "At the seminary, I wear a sweatshirt given to me by my Catholic siblings. Printed on the front is 'Father Sister'." Since Margie decided to cut loose and start her long trek toward a new career, she has learned how to confront and solve a host of problems, not too unlike those she faces in the ministry.

From the Auctioneer's Block

An important linchpin in Hugh Hildesley's career in the ministry is that nothing in life is ever wasted. This is a lesson that applies to nearly all career changers. Now, as rector of the Church of the Heavenly Rest on New York's East Side, Hugh (early fifties) enjoys his past experience as an art appraiser and senior executive at Sotheby's, the international art appraisers and auctioneers, with the duties of an Episcopal priest.

Born in England, he left Oxford University after one year and in 1961 while in his early twenties became an apprentice at Sotheby's London headquarters. Three years later, Hugh was transferred to the company's New York City office as a collector and auctioneer. During the next 10 years, he became an expert in Dutch old master paintings.

His boyhood dream of becoming a priest returned when he was in his early thirties. By then, Hugh was married with several young children. There were, however, a number of academic roadblocks. He lacked the credentials to qualify for seminary admission. Even though his bishop tried to discourage him by citing education costs and family responsibilities, he recommended him for a special work-study program at the Cathedral of St. John the Divine Institute of Theology.

The bishop cautioned that "if you're really interested in the church and your calling is 'true,' you'll have every opportunity to be tested." His warning proved to be accurate. To Hugh, it meant giving up all social life, attending courses on evenings and weekends, never getting more than five hours sleep a night, and, in tandem with his heavy Sotheby's travel schedule, studying on airplanes and in airports and hotel rooms.

Ordained in 1977, Hugh served the next six years as a replacement priest at several local parishes, including Heavenly Rest. He was also promoted to senior vice president at Sotheby's. The *pro bono publico* (for the public good) life of a "weekend priest" was insufficient challenge. His fortunes changed in 1983, when the rector at Heavenly Rest resigned. After searching for nearly one year, Hugh was "called" as the rector of a church with nearly 2000 parishioners. This meant a drastic cut in income, one he admits he never expects to overcome.

Don't be mistaken: Hugh's nontraditional entry into the ministry troubled some parishioners. At a church the size of Heavenly Rest, they normally employ a "seasoned" rector. Hugh got the job because of his apprenticeship at the church and his business experience. The congregation recognized the need for rector with the combined skills of spiritual advisor and business manager.

Then came the hard work. He had to learn how to administer a church, including the supervision of a full-time staff of 12 and $1 million budget.

He was shocked by some aspects of his new lifestyle. "People thought that ministers wrote with a quill pen. There wasn't even an electric typewriter in the office. Of course, I changed all that by computerizing the entire operation."

His 20 years as an art historian and corporate manager have also come in handy. "Much of Flemish and Dutch art has religious settings. They provide a rich visual image of the Bible which I reference in my sermons. As the head of Sotheby's trusts and estates, I was used to advising people in distress. And as a career switcher, I counsel a number of parishioners who have lost their jobs and are looking for new opportunities."

Tales from a Former Headhunter

Lee Smith's (midfifties) biography reads like a corporate success story. At 39, he was the executive vice president and a major shareholder in one of the nation's first publicly owned executive search firms. His specialty was Wall Street. Lee had worked nearly 20 years in the financial field, starting with a part-time job at Merrill Lynch & Company, Inc. while attending college.

As a search firm executive, Lee lived the good life. He could easily afford tailor-made suits, a cooperative apartment on Park Avenue in Manhattan, a country home in the Berkshire Mountains in upstate New York, and regular first-class vacation trips to Europe. He was the mid-1970s version of a yuppie.

Outwardly there was little reason for Lee ever to consider changing careers, yet in 1974 he walked away from Wall Street and his idyllic life to become a Roman Catholic priest. He knew that he had achieved one level of success, but deep down he wanted to help people in a significant way. "It was the hardest decision in my life since I felt I had a meaningful career and enjoyed a happy life. But, I got the calling. As an expert in placing people, I was hardly running away. I wanted to use these same skills in a different way by working with a wider range of people. It was time to change careers."

The Church welcomes new priests, but there is also a degree of skepticism and uncertainty about midlife career changes. It conducts interviews and psychological tests to affirm an applicant's dedication and to weed out romantics. After meeting the standards, Lee studied for three years at Pope John the XXIII, a seminary in Massachusetts and one of several in the United States that specializes in training older seminarians. He then spent several years as a parish priest in New York City before receiving his current assignment in the mid-1980s as chaplain at the Stella Maris Seaman Center in Brooklyn's Red Hook section, a neighborhood reminiscent of scenes in the film *On the Waterfront*.

From his office, which overlooks New York's lower harbor and is directly across the river from Wall Street, Lee serves a wandering congregation—cargo and containership sailors who spend at most a few days in the New York harbor while their ships unload, load, and refuel. "They live a lonely life at sea, and contrary to their image, most sailors in port just want to call home, play pool, relax, and buy a few things for the ship. Some even seek my advice."

As a priest, Lee, constantly draws upon past business experiences. In executive search work, one counsels clients and based on their skills, matches them with an appropriate job. This background is ideally suited to a priest.

"I've been a broker in people my entire adult life. On Wall Street, I learned the importance of letting clients know exactly how they stood and that there was no hidden agenda. This approach also applies to sailors and parishioners who are usually suspicious of a priest's motives."

Retailer Turned Priest

The Roman Catholic Church needs priests with business experience to work at the parish level. Managing a church or, in fact, any religious institution is a complex matter. As we've already discovered, Lee Smith provides an array of strong business credentials. Martin Kline (early fifties), who was ordained in 1991, offers a different set of credentials from Lee Smith's. Before deciding to become a priest, Marty spent several years planning the move.

After 25 years of retail experience as a jewelry buyer and the operations manager of one of Long Island's largest shopping centers, it took Marty four years to make the transition from business to the seminary. These years gave him the time to fully comprehend the enormity of his move.

He quit his retail job and completed his undergraduate degree. To meet expenses he worked as the business manager of a local parish—one with a $1 million operating budget. Martin, the businessman, knows Lotus 1-2-3 and spread sheet analysis, but Martin, the priest, wants to avoid being known as a business manager-priest. "To me, business is just one more skill that today's parish priest needs to run a church."

The Lawyer Becomes a Rabbi

Being trained in advocacy is in many ways an ideal skill for a career in the clergy since oral and written presentations are critical to effective religious leadership. Joshua Hoffer Skoff (early thirties), although a younger career switcher than most, was a litigation and securities lawyer with a Chicago firm before entering the Jewish Theological Seminary.

"Corporate law was good to me, but I was more interested in community service and teaching. Occasional *pro bono* assignments weren't satisfying enough." When he decided to switch, Josh was advised by his rabbi father on the pluses and minuses of a rabbinical career. As an associate rabbi earning over $50,000 a year in salary and benefits at a suburban Cleveland synagogue, Josh continues to utilize his legal skills.

"Rabbis and lawyers both have to read and interpret vast amounts of materials, and they rely on direct relationships with people. Above all, they require that 'clients' trust the rabbi or lawyer's confidentiality and judgment."

From Advertising Copywriter to Rabbi

Unlike Joshua Skoff, Rabbi Loraine Heller (late thirties) received little family guidance in making her career change. A Californian, she came to New York after graduating from college and then worked for more than six years as a medical copywriter at several advertising agencies. "I got to the point in my career where executive search firms were calling me at home, but even with professional recognition, there wasn't enough job satisfaction."

Loraine reasoned that being a rabbi would combine her interests in Judaism and in helping people. After resigning her agency job, she spent two semesters at New York University, taking courses in religion and preparing for the five-year academic program at the Hebrew Union College–Jewish Institute of Religion. When she entered the seminary in the mid-1980s, women were by then readily accepted and ordained as Reform rabbis.

To pay seminary costs, she used student loans and savings and lived modestly in an inexpensive East Side apartment. Ordained in 1990, Loraine, like other women rabbis, deliberately avoided a pastoral assignment and instead accepted a position as staff chaplain at a large Jewish home for the aged. Earning approximately $40,000, somewhat less than she might have made as an assistant rabbi in a synagogue, she attends to the religious needs of 800 residents. Unlike most career switchers, she finds that many of her past business credentials have little carryover value, yet she admits that "good advertising copy and a sermon both have to capture attention."

Married with Children

For potential career changers who believe they already have too many obligations, William Stokes (midthirties) appears to have taken many of life's obligations in stride. Responsibility does not seem to conflict with Bill and his clerical ambitions. Between the time he completed two years of college and a decade later when he entered the General Theological Seminary, he married; had four children; became the legal guardian for his nephew; waited on tables, bartended, and managed a number of Baltimore, Houston, and New York City restaurants; and returned to complete undergraduate courses, taking 48 credits in three semesters.

Bill decided to fulfill his dream and become an Episcopal priest when he found that there "was more to life than the bottom line. My mission is to help people understand who they are."

During this whirlwind period before entering the seminary, he and his wife, Susan, held several series of jobs to save enough money so they would be free of debt while Bill was a seminarian. Once he was a student, the hectic schedule continued. Bill managed the seminary's refectory, and Susan worked full-time as a hotel supervisor.

Now assigned to a Long Island church as a curate earning in the mid-$20,000s, he finds that restaurant work was actually ideal training for the ministry. "I'm used to the irregular hours and working with all types of people: waiters, cooks, bartenders, kitchen help, suppliers, and customers. They teach you about human nature."

Transition from the Executive Suite

While William Stokes was building family responsibility during his twenties, the Reverend Betty Hudson (early forties) was acquiring strong corporate credentials. After leaving her Texas home following graduation from Tulane University, Betty worked in Boston for several years as a computer programmer, received an MBA from Simmons College, and in 1976 joined Exxon Corporation's financial staff in New York City.

Seven years later, when her base pay was $65,000, she resigned to become an Episcopal priest. As a rector, she now earns $29,000 in salary plus a home at no cost but worth about $2000 a month in tax benefits.

"I'll never again match my Exxon salary. Looking around, I realized that hundreds of people at Exxon could just as easily have done my job. I wanted to make a unique contribution. I had reached a point where I had proved that I could make it as a woman in the corporate world."

With severance pay and the proceeds from selling her midtown apartment, she financed part of her theological training. Midway through the three-year seminary program, she married John, an accountant. His financial support is critical since most Protestant clergy need a second adult's income to survive financially.

Her first assignment after ordination in 1986 at St. Stephen's in Pearl River, New York (about 30 miles north of New York City) ended five years later. It was her objective to have her own congregation. It was not a matter of discrimination that she was not named rector at St. Stephen's, but rather it is in keeping with a diocesan policy that discourages elevating the interim rector to rector. Even so, it was one year before she was called as Grace's rector.

The Episcopal Church has been ordaining women for over 15 years, but many parishes are still uncomfortable about having a woman rector. Her experiences were more favorable than "Barbara Miller's." In job interviews, Betty found it was similar to job interviewing she experienced in industry a decade ago.

Parish interview committees seek women superperformers. In Betty's case, they appreciated that she had an MBA. She declined several interviews when she learned that "they were not ready as yet for a woman rector." In one instance, she was a finalist, losing out to another woman who was a seminary classmate.

During several other interviews, she was pleasantly surprised to find that over half the screening committee consisted of working women like herself. One of these churches, Grace Episcopal in Hastings-on-Hudson, called her to become its rector.

Betty, however, continues to miss some aspects of corporate life, especially the ready accessibility of automated equipment. "Most parishes are at least 10 years behind business in applying computers to solve everyday administrative problems. At St. Stephen's, I wrote my sermons and pastoral letters on a home laptop computer since there was no office computer. At Grace Episcopal, we at least have a PC."

A Jazz Trombonist's Gig in the Pulpit

In the traditional sense, Michael Cobbler (early forties) could hardly be categorized as a typical *Second Act* career changer. He moved from music and music education to the Lutheran ministry within a few years of graduating from the Peabody Conservatory in Baltimore. Yet his career is rich in diverse experiences, and he has meshed two different professional worlds in a single career.

"While I was in high school in New York, I was selected as a trombonist in the all-city orchestra. I was raised as a Christian Scientist, but a friend in the orchestra interested me in Lutheranism and I converted. I wanted to be a professional musician but dropped out of the Manhattan School of Music when I ran out of money. Thinking of myself as a hotshot trombonist, I was a clerk at New York Life Insurance during the day and did club dates at night. For a short time, I saw little reason to go to college."

Mike's life took a more positive turn when he found that his musical career was limited without a sound musical education.

He was recommended and received a nearly full scholarship to attend the Peabody Conservatory in Baltimore.

Over the next three years, he made extra money playing in jazz and rock bands and as a classical musician with the Baltimore Symphony Orchestra. Because he is an African-American, he was conscious of the difficulties for minorities in getting jobs with a symphony orchestra. As a practical solution, he majored in music education. Mike then taught music for several years in the Baltimore school system and also performed with pop and jazz bands and symphony orchestras.

"The hounds of heaven started barking, and I learned there was a place in the church for musicians. No reason I couldn't praise the Lord with my trombone. I was advised that music could be part of my ministry. While I attended Lutheran Theology Seminary, I was playing in bands. Music would be the thread in my ministry. It brings people together. Nearly everyone likes some form of music and can relate whether it is rock or the classics."

Following ordination, he was transferred from parish to parish—three years in Philadelphia; four years in Camden, New Jersey, followed by two years in another New Jersey church, where he shared the pulpit with his wife, Thelma, also an ordained Lutheran minister. In 1990, Mike moved to New York City to head a church coalition working with inner city Lutheran congregations.

---◆---

Points to Remember

► Besides a spiritual involvement, the clergy of all denominations are concerned with social issues.

► The job market is somewhat sluggish for the Protestant clergy.

► All religions encourage midlife career changers.

► A second income in the family is needed to balance the books.

► It takes three to five years of seminary study to be ordained.

► The pay has improved for rabbis but is still depressed for the Protestant clergy.

► Women continue to suffer from lower pay and fewer opportunities.

---◆---

CHAPTER 13

Community Service and Psychological Services

CAREER OPPORTUNITIES IN COMMUNITY SERVICE

We're a nation of joiners and doers. To most people, volunteer firefighting or acting as a trustee of a nonprofit organization is little more than an extracurricular activity. A number of career changers have taken the next step, however. They have exchanged volunteerism for a full-time second career in social and community action programs.

An estimated 400,000 professional social workers are employed by government agencies (relatively few in the federal government) and in private agencies, such as hospitals, mental health facilities, community and religious organizations, schools and youth groups, and voluntary self-help organizations.

According to the National Association of Social Workers, the representatives for 140,000 professionals, 80,000 of its members work in full- or part-time clinical positions and about 22,000 in private practice.

Social workers are often the foot soldiers in community service organizations. In return for their hands-on professional contribution, more times than not they are underpaid. Even social workers with master degrees and doctorates earn lower entry-level and later salaries than comparable professionals in other fields.

The pressures to reduce government and nonprofit social services tend to undermine job security. Dramatizing the social workers' plight is the fallout from the recent survey conducted in Pennsylvania: those serving the needy are increasingly becoming impoverished themselves, often earning about the same wages as supermarket and theater ticket clerks.

The U.S. Bureau of Labor Statistics indicates that employment of social workers is expected to increase faster than the average for all occupations over the next decade to replace workers who leave the field and to handle the growing caseload among individuals and families in crisis.

Approximately 375 colleges provide undergraduate degrees in social work: 100 award a master degree and another 50, a doctorate. Licensing or certification is not mandatory for most staff jobs, although some form of licensing or registration is required in 46 states to work in private practice.

THE CAREER SWITCHERS

From Advertising Sales to Social Service Worker

When one thinks of a social worker, Mary McCormick's (late forties) job as a case worker fits the description.

Mary faced a career decision in 1989 when she lost her job as the advertising director of a popular consumer magazine. With 20 years of experience with advertising agencies and consumer magazines, she was named advertising director of *McCall's Needlework & Crafts Magazine* in 1988.

She lost her job a year later when McCall's cut staff to balance the budget. Do you prepare a resume and look for a related job? How realistic is it to expect to find similar work?

She looked for other advertising jobs, but she soon realized that employers could just as easily hire two people, although somewhat less trained than herself, for the salary she was asking. This is a problem that affects other midlife executives who have reached the upper salary range in their professions. What steps do they take when the next move is checkmate?

Starting in college, where she was a sociology major, Mary was interested in social work. As part of her job search, she began to read employment ads for social workers. Replying to a *New York Times* classified ad, she was hired the next day by Catholic Charities Diocese of Brooklyn.

Mary is assigned to a neighborhood field office advising senior citizens. She serves as their advocate with government and social agencies and helps them obtain vital services, such as Medicare or home nursing care. Her former Madison Avenue milieu and the Brooklyn streets are worlds apart, yet she often uses her communications skills to convince the elderly to apply for social service benefits or to move into a nursing home.

Leaving the business world was difficult, starting with a severe pay cut and the disappearance of enjoyable business trips and corporate entertainment. Mary reduced her living expenses, and to offset her lower income she dipped into savings.

In keeping with her longer term career objectives, she plans to relocate to the Southwest, where living costs are less, there is a need for professionals to work with the area's growing senior citizen population, and she can earn a master degree at $45 a credit.

Operating a Street-Corner Mission

Mary McCormick works as a traditional case worker, but Geoffrey Worden's (early fifties) career as a community activist has taken an entirely different twist. Why, in fact, would an investment banker want to work one-on-one with the homeless?

Worden severed a 26-year career at Kidder Peabody & Company, Inc. for a life that blends religious conviction with the need to help the homeless cope with everyday living. No longer a Wall Street investment banker, Geoff plans to get more people involved with Bridge, the street-corner mission that he began several years ago. Through a business alliance that he also formed, Geoff is helping minorities buy into and run their own companies.

As soon as Geoff received an MBA from Harvard University in the mid-1960s, he joined Kidder Peabody. Ten years later, at 35, he was named comanager of the firm's investment banking department and he married Virginia, a corporate lawyer, also working on Wall Street. His career and personal life were shaping into the prototypic Wall Street success story.

Geoff's concern for social causes is deeply rooted. "I need more involvement than writing a check to support a good cause or being elected to a board of trustees. If I'm going to help people, I want to work directly with them." In today's vernacular, this is hands-on experience.

His career changeover started in the late 1980s, when Geoff, who took a year's partial leave of absence to study at the Union Theological Seminary, started to respond personally to the homeless.

"I looked the homeless in the eye and just couldn't walk by. I could have continued to stay as a second-rate theologian and even been ordained, but I decided that the world could use some elbow grease in the form of a street outreach program."

At this point, Virginia and Geoff's organizational ability, along with their business and social contacts, paid off. Still employed at Kidder Peabody as an investment specialist in the energy industry, Bridge was launched with the specific objective to distribute food, clothing, blankets, and other practical items to several hundred homeless in the lower part of Manhattan. Supplies, funds, and volunteers primarily come from Summit, New Jersey, where the Wordens and many of their Wall Street associates live.

"Being practical, we chose the homeless who live in and around Wall Street. That's where we work and that's where we have our first responsibility."

Bridge makes its distribution every Friday evening from the back of station wagons that tour lower Manhattan. Over the past year, the Wordens have stepped back from Bridge's day-to-day operations. It is their way to ensure that the organization builds additional leadership and is not identified exclusively with the Worden family.

In defining Bridge's mission, Geoff found that "we knew our business and suburban world but we knew little about the homeless and their needs. We had to adapt to their world."

"When we found that they had terrible teeth, we replaced apples with easier to chew tangerines and bananas. We talked the Oral-B Corporation into selling us 2000 toothbrushes at cost. Bridge has distributed over 45,000 meals, and we've involved several thousand people in some phase of the program, most of whom would never had any relationship with the homeless. But we do more than pass out supplies. As a street-corner ministry, we talk to the homeless and try to help them in some small way with their everyday problems of survival."

Self-help for the Homeless

Like Geoff Worden, Gene Estess (midfifties) is a product of Wall Street. Also like Geoff, Gene has identified his second career with New York's homeless.

Gene grew up in Rock Island, Illinois, graduated from the University of Pennsylvania Wharton School. He worked for 8 years in the family's retail stores in the Midwest, and then moved to New York where, over the next 23 years, he was employed by several brokerage and investment banking firms.

By the mid-1980s, the homeless had become a noticeable social problem. Their presence was no longer restricted to a cluster of outlying neighborhoods.

"I could not ignore the homeless. At the same time, I began to become even more ambivalent about working on Wall Street. There was a chunk missing in my life. Like many people my age, I was tied to the past, including a high salary. At my wife's request, I even went for career counseling to establish my priorities."

The impetus to do something different started in 1985. Gene, then a daily railroad commuter, regularly passed the same homeless woman in Grand Central Station. Instead of ignoring her plea, he started to help her financially.

In a companion move, he became a volunteer with the Jericho Project, a nonprofit group with a unique formula to help the homeless become self-sufficient. Operating from a West Side apartment house, the Jericho Project offers housing, counseling, and job referals to homeless men and women who must also be recovering alcoholics or addicts.

Soon afterward, he joined the Jericho Project's board. Within two years, the organization was recruiting a new director and Gene applied for the job. If he was hired, this meant leaving Wall Street, a steep cut in pay, and a need to dip into investments to meet living expenses. Some board members objected that Gene had neither a degree in social work nor appropriate professional credentials. Despite the critics, he was hired as director and soon demonstrated that work skills that may seem unrelated can be transferable.

"When I left Wall Street, some business associates thought I had flipped. Others were at a loss for words but thought that I would do something like this sooner than later." In response to the increasing homeless population, Gene has extended the Jericho Project's reach into two other neighborhoods in New York City and has doubled its residential and one-on-one services to nearly 160 clients. Most other social agencies are almost totally dependent on the shrinking pool of government funds for support, but the Jericho Project receives 85 percent of its funding from private sources. Gene runs it as a business.

"As a one-time salesman, I apply these skills in fund-raising and negotiations with corporate management. If anything, the Jericho Project lets me live every fantasy that I ever had."

Applying One's Own Physical Disability in a New Career

After 30 years, Stephen Janick's (early fifties) career is coming full circle, not from careful career planning but rather as a result of an accident that left him a quadriplegic when he was 32 years old. This event reshaped his career.

When Steve graduated in the early 1960s from Lake Forest College in Illinois, his career might have moved in any one of three directions: social worker, Harvard University Divinity School student and a career as a Presbyterian minister, or business. He selected business and joined Libby McNeil & Libby (now owned by Nestlé) as a package goods marketer. Even with his interest in community activism, sales and marketing had an even greater appeal.

In the late 1960s, Libby gave him a year's leave of absence to study at the Massachusetts Institute of Technology. "My prime area of interest at MIT was strategic analysis and strategic choices. Little did I realize that the academic lessons would apply so directly in my future career." Two years after returning to Libby, Janick joined Bristol-Myers Company (now Bristol-Myers Squibb Company), where he became vice president and general manager of the Domesticare Division.

As Steve climbed the executive ladder he became disenchanted with the corporate life, but he was unwilling to trade in the fast track for a different lifestyle. Fate stepped in. Tragedy struck in 1974, when Steve became a quadriplegic after a freak swimming pool accident.

After nine months in rehabilitation, he returned to Domesticare. During this period, sensitivity to the needs of the disabled took priority over his corporate career.

He left Domesticare and for the next nine years served as a full-time, independent representative for the handicapped. His advocacy was recognized with an appointment as director of the New Jersey Division of Rehabilitation, a position he has held under two governors. "I discovered a world of people with disabilities. I had never been associated with people who had problems like that, and it opened up a whole new set of challenges."

As a marketer, he was trained to define his market, relate it to the company's mission, and work to gain a consensus before introducing a new product. Steve applies the techniques of strategic analysis and strategic choices, which he learned at MIT, to the identification and development of more opportunities for the disabled.

During his second career, which has now been nearly as long as the career in consumer marketing, Steve has not forgotten an earlier interest in the ministry. He's starting to consider a third career, this time attending theology school to study the Old and New Testaments.

Dancer Turns Court Translator

When Carmen Barros (early forties) told friends that she was giving up dancing for a career as a translator, a few called her a "traitor" for trading in the arts for such a pedestrian career. But

Carmen followed a course taken by many career switchers, one that begins with a candid evaluation of one's capabilities. Based on this process, Carmen decided on a career that integrates social commitment and professional skills.

Other than a few dance luminaries, Carmen knew the career limitations facing most middle-aged dancers. Even though she had danced with the Ballet Hispanico of New York and danced in a number of commercials on Spanish television, Carmen questioned her own future as a professional dancer. A single mother with two young children, Carmen was looking for long-term career opportunities along with greater financial security. A career-counseling course stimulated her to use her language skills as a court translator and to form Inter-National Interpreters and Translators.

Although her company handles translating assignments in most languages, the demographics of metropolitan New York provide the social challenges. She represents disadvantaged Hispanics in Spanish and Haitians in French before the Social Security Administration, workers' compensation boards, jails, and hospitals, all of which are required by law to provide and pay for translation services.

"There are parallels between dancing and translating. In dancing one exercises, warms up, and practices every day. It is a mandatory discipline. As a dancer, I performed under pressure before an audience. So does the translator. And, the dancer's attention to detail and total concentration can only be matched by being a court translator." This is so intense that some court assignments require that translators operate in shifts, working 20 to 30 minutes at a time.

A Jesuit Educator Finds a New Career

When Herbert Hezel (late fifties) was 17, he took the first step leading to ordination as a Jesuit priest. Other than a six-year period in the 1960s when he was studying in the United States, Hezel spent 20 years as a Jesuit teacher and school administrator in the Philippines. During this period, he also received a master degree and a doctorate in educational administration from St. Thomas University in Manila.

He climbed the educational ladder in the Philippines as a teacher, supervisor of English for nine Jesuit high schools, and assistant and then superintendent of the nation's entire Jesuit elementary through university school system.

In his early forties, Hezel's Jesuit career was on hold. In conflict with Roman Catholic Church dogma and the issue of celibacy, he left the Philippines and the Jesuits and returned to the United States, where he started looking for a "civilian" job.

He had extensive administrative experience, but he really didn't know how to relate education to the U.S. business world. Since he could type 65 words a minute, he worked as an office temporary to support himself while looking for work.

From a *Business Week Magazine* article, he learned about outplacement, then a comparatively new management service. He liked the concept. It required professionals with his kind of experience, and it had a social objective in trying to help people. "It also seemed like a field where there is lots of variety. Whenever possible, I try to avoid taking the same road twice." He was hired by Orr, Cuthrell Fuchs Associates, Inc. (now Fuchs, Cuthrell & Company, Inc.).

He spent nearly 16 years with the firm, becoming senior executive vice president and supervisor for the firm's multioffice network. In late 1991, he left Fuchs, Cuthrell and joined the Labor Education Community Service Agency to counsel dislocated workers.

"Religious training and my own search for work were actually good experiences for outplacement consulting. I know how to counsel people with problems, and I can help others travel the difficult road in planning their own careers."

A Deep Social Obligation

"When I was in the position to pay back for my good fortunes, I believed it was my social responsibility to return something to society." This is the way that Marvin Lender (early fifties) describes his full-time work as a community activist and board chairman of the United Jewish Appeal.

Some people dream about dedicating more time to social causes; Marvin Lender started his public service career when he was in his midforties. The opportunity presented itself in 1984, when he and his brother, Murray, sold Lender's Bagels Bakery Inc. to Kraft Inc., which at that time had been merged into the General Foods Corporation and was called Kraft General Foods Inc., now a subsidiary of the Philip Morris Companies. Lender's Bagels had grown in 37 years to a $65 million bakery and was a national distributor.

The Kraft acquisition represented a once-in-a-lifetime opportunity for Marvin, 43, and his brother, 10 years older. They used the proceeds to form M&M Investments to manage their portfolio. M&M gave him the opportunity to apply his management skills to a number of community service organizations in his hometown, New Haven, Connecticut, and on a national level to the UJA.

"I'm essentially a fund-raiser, spending about 90 percent of my time on UJA and other nonprofit work. I look at public service work as the most important thing I've ever done. In running a family-owned business, I was involved in every phase of the company's operations. It's my management style. Now I dedicate the same effort to non-profit and community work."

The marketing techniques that were used in making Lender's Bagels a national name are applied in fund-raising—with one exception. "In non-profit work, I've come to accept the idea that I'm now dealing exclusively with human lives."

CAREER OPPORTUNITIES IN PSYCHOLOGICAL SERVICES

Psychologists are in demand as mediators, counselors, testers, and analysts to help solve individual, family, and intragroup societal problems. Of the nation's more than 125,000 practicing psychologists, 40 percent are self-employed. According to the U.S. Bureau of Labor Statistics, about one-third work for educational institutions, a similar number in health care facilities, 16 percent for government, and the balance of industry. This is a field that appeals to midlife career changers because there is a correlation between life experience and the ability to offer sound counseling.

Lack of sufficient academic and professional credentials need not discourage career changers. Nearly every U.S. undergraduate college offers courses in psychology. Good jobs and long-term career opportunities realistically start with a master degree, and a doctorate is almost mandatory for supervisory jobs, college teaching, and in consulting.

The American Psychological Association, the guardian of the profession, monitors both PhD and doctor of psychology programs. In a quasi-medical field, the title "doctor" furnishes the needed professional cachet and, more importantly, enables private-practice psychologists to meet state licensing requirements.

The job market, says the U.S. Bureau of Labor Statistics, is expected to grow over the next 10 years, stimulated by an increasing demand for psychologists to work in programs related to the family and to alcohol abuse, drug dependency, and other social problems. Psychologists have a strong attachment to the profession, with only a relatively small number exiting the field each year.

Salaries to a large extent are based on the number of degrees and the place of employment—government agency, educational institution, industry, or private practice. Salaries, for entrants with a doctorate range from $24,000 to $54,000, reports the American Psychological Association. Some business and industrial psychologists, including self-employed practitioners, earn up to $120,000.

THE CAREER SWITCHERS

Husband and Wife Have Separate Practices

Meet Stan Harrison (early sixties) and Toni Heris (late fifties). They have a lot in common. Besides being husband and wife, they are psychologists, career switchers from retail advertising, and recipients of doctorates in the mid-1980s from New York University.

As professionals in the same field, they share ideas and concepts, yet by design they have separate offices and different specialties; Stan in biofeedback and stress management, Tony in career development. They met in the late 1960s at a retail advertising conference sponsored jointly by NYU and the *New York Times* and were married several years later.

After both lost their jobs, they became freelance advertising copywriters. They earned a good living, but they also had time on their hands. How would they spend the time to their mutual advantage? They considered various career alternatives.

Neither wanted to start an advertising agency, nor did they want to manage and run a business. They shared a love-hate relationship with advertising, but they admit it paid the bills.

Then in their early forties, Stan asked, What courses could we take to improve our skills, and how in the long run can we become professionals who are independent of corporate salaries and pressures?

This was not the first time that Stan had such professional dreams. Since college, he had a secret desire to work in academia, but in a family in which he was the first person ever to go to college, the idea of also going to graduate school was not feasible. Toni always wanted to be a writer, but like Stan, advertising copywriting was a way to get a job.

As freelance copywriters, they had ample time to structure a realistic plan that would lead in 10 years to doctorates in psychology, professional certification, and their own consulting practices.

As newcomers entering the profession in their midfifties, they found their age to be a distinct advantage because patients often equate age with wisdom. Reflecting on the transition from advertising to psychology, Stan admits that a number of the skills learned in advertising copywriting are useful in dealing with patients. Both fields call for an ability to work with words and, often, abstract concepts. In other ways, a psychology practice has little relationship to advertising.

"In advertising, you meet with a client at 10 a.m., and that afternoon you complete the first draft of the copy. The pace is much slower and results take longer to achieve in psychology." As former copywriters, however, they act like the cobbler with his children: neither uses advertising to attract new patients.

From TV Writer to Psychotherapy

On a shelf in Paul Mayer's (early sixties) small study, where he meets patients, there are eight Emmy Award trophies, all in recognition of *"Ryan's Hope,"* a syndicated afternoon TV serial that he coauthored and coproduced with Claire Labine from 1975 through 1980.

Paul always wanted to be a writer, and he entered the field when he graduated from Harvard College in 1949. Over the next 20 years, he held a series of jobs and was a freelance writer of U.S. Army educational films and off-Broadway plays.

"I could never work successfully at a full-time corporate job since I have trouble with authority figures. What's more, I never liked working for others."

In 1970, he and his wife, Sasha von Scherler, an actress, and like Paul a recent career switcher into psychotherapy (see Chapter 2), gave a large dinner party. As fate would have it, a guest who knew Paul was a writer asked him to submit a sample TV script. The invitation resulted in his first daytime serial, *"Where the Heart Is."*

This was also the start of a 13-year collaboration with Claire Labine and their creation of *"Ryan's Hope."* The serial was enormously successful, and Paul enjoyed every moment even though it meant writing 265 half-hour scripts a year and over 1500 scripts during the life of the show. He worked every day and a minimum of five nights a week in writing and production. During their first three years, Paul and Claire had an independent contractual relationship with the American Broadcasting Company. A change in the network's management resulted in some corporate interference during the last two years of the series.

"In the TV business, the name of the game is to create the product, own the program, and then sell it. When ABC cancelled *"Ryan's Hope"* in 1980, the rights reverted to Claire and me and we also won syndication rights in Europe."

Finding a sequel to this TV success story was rather difficult. In search of fresh ideas, Paul moved to Los Angeles. He lived a Hollywood lifestyle: a house with a swimming pool and a view of the San Fernando Valley. He had little luck in creating another network winner, however. He jokingly said to a therapist friend that he'd like to get out of TV. She replied, "Why not?"

Paul returned to New York, where he researched the possibility of becoming a psychologist. He wanted to know if he was too old to enter the field. If not, how could he do it and should he get a doctorate? Five years of study for the PhD seemed too long and costly. A master of social work represented a faster way to become a licensed therapist.

By the time Paul received his degree and studied psychoanalysis for four more years, he had invested several hundred thousand dollars of his savings to establish himself in a career in which he earns about $60,000 a year.

Stan Harrison and Toni Heris studiously avoid using advertising to attract patients, but Paul is more aggressive. He actively seeks writers and actors as patients since he instinctively understands their needs. About 75 percent of his patients, who pay between $75 and $90 an hour, are writers, graphic artists, and designers.

In addition to referrals, he attracts patients by identifying with his past TV successes. One small ad in a neighborhood weekly newspaper says, "Psychotherapy to Creative people . . . writers block, performance anxiety, self-destructive choices, despair . . . by Emmy Winner" and Paul's telephone number.

———————◆———————

Points to Remember

► Social workers are the foot soldiers in community relations work.

► Comparatively low pay is of prime concern and an employment issue.

► There is a good job market for social workers.

► There's more to the social work field than being a caseworker.

► Psychologists earn dividends when they have a doctorate.

► About 40 percent of psychologists are self-employed.

———————◆———————

CHAPTER 14

Retail and Service Businesses

CAREER OPPORTUNITIES IN RETAILING

If you play the averages, then retailing is not for you. Credit rating agencies like Dun & Bradstreet, Inc. report that failures among retail and service businesses is nearing an all-time high.

To begin, it's best to understand why so many retail businesses fail. The United States is becoming "overstored." Downtowns, small towns, the suburbs, or the omnipresent shopping malls, independents and boutiques are fighting it out with the chains and mass merchandisers for the same sales dollar. This type of competitive environment takes its toll.

Don't be discouraged. The career changers you meet in this chapter knew the odds when they went into business. Before they committed to opening a retail or service business, they carefully planned their new venture, using many of the marketing tools they acquired in their former corporate jobs. They took precautions. Nearly all avoided competing head-on with the mass marketers. Instead they become niche specialists. A few even failed and took different directions in their careers.

THE CAREER SWITCHERS

The Environmental Retailers

Until mid-1991, Stefan Doering (late twenties) and Ned Geeslin (early thirties) were corporate up-and-comers. They were well educated and married and had jobs with major organizations. Stefan, who has an MBA, was working as a computer systems specialist at Citibank, and Ned, the son of a newspaper reporter, was a senior editor of Time-Warner, Inc.'s highly successful *Entertainment Weekly*.

Then the walls came tumbling down. Stefan lost his Citibank job as the bank downsized, but he had already started to look for a career that would combine his interests in business and the environment. Coincidentally, he joined a food cooperative in Brooklyn, which stimulated him to consider opening a retail store that sold only environmentally sound products.

Stefan placed a classified ad in the food coop's newsletter announcing his business plans. Ned, who had become disinterested in reporting entertainment news, left his editing job the same week Stefan's ad appeared.

From the outset, the relationship between Stefan and Ned was fundamentally sound. Stefan had a business plan and a group of investors; Ned had already been collecting information on environmental products. Several months later, Earth General was born in Park Slope, an upscale Brooklyn community where residents support environmental issues. As Brooklyn residents, both partners knew the area. Until then, environmental merchandise was available only from catalogs or from one other New York City specialty store.

Other than when Stefan worked part-time as a teenager in his grandfather's general store in Delta, Colorado, neither partner had any previous retail experience. Since Earth General was to be a one-of-a-kind store, they decided to learn about retailing on the job. Stefan developed a computer system to track merchandise, keep records, and house the mailing list.

More importantly, both shared the view that the store should sell basic merchandise to area residents at a price competitive with merchandise sold by the other local merchants. In their 750-square-foot store, they stock toilet paper, tissues, soap, and office supplies made from recycled paper; wallets and handbags made of recycled rubber but with the feel of leather; T-shirts and children's jumpsuits produced from untreated cotton; and earrings made from recycled materials. They also carry environmental books and indoor gardening supplies.

Six months after it opened, Earth General is operating on a break-even basis, eased somewhat because both partners are being supported by working wives. Stefan and Ned already plan to expand the Earth General concept. They are looking for additional store sites with favorable demographics and to increase the scope of their current catalog.

Leaves Sears and Opens Her Own Store

Before buying the Crocus Hill Market in St. Paul in 1990, Karen Glance (midthirties) worked nearly 15 years in the high-pressure mass merchandising field. She moved from New York to Minnesota when the Sears Roebuck and Company Pinstripe Petite Division recruited her as a vice president and director of store operations.

Although the salary was excellent, she was working at least 65 hours a week and traveling extensively. She had little time to enjoy her new lifestyle. Pinstripe, during downsizing 30 months later, allowed Karen to execute her golden parachute. With the proceeds, she bought the Crocus Hill Market. Her goal was to transform a turn-of-the-century store into a specialty grocery store serving an upscale St. Paul clientele.

Karen's business plan, although sound in many ways, fell short of its objective. The store attracted new customers and sales often exceeded $10,000 a week, but expenses got out of hand.

She discovered that many of the store's long-time, home delivery, charge account customers took 60 days to pay their bills. And retail sales fell sharply when they moved during the summer months to their vacation homes.

When Karen bought Crocus Hill she was featured on a number of local TV programs. One interview attracted the attention of the owner of a gourmet delicatessen and grocery store on Lake Minnetonka. The owner was also a real estate developer who had remodeled the food store but wanted to concentrate on home building.

Sales volume at Crocus Hill continued to be sluggish. Even so, Karen bought the 1500-square-foot Cottingwood General Store, the only store situated in the midst of a high-income residential area. The 100-year-old store, which predates nearly all the homes, is protected by the local grandfather laws.

By October 1991, Karen realized that Crocus Hill had serious operating problems. They could be corrected, but rather than refinance the store she took a "sizable" loss and closed down. At this time, Karen, now the owner of Cottingwood, could easily have returned to chain store retailing. Search firms had approached her, but she decided to continue to be her own boss.

"As a Sears executive, there were the expected corporate pressures. Why didn't branch stores take their sales quotas for the week? No excuses for bad weather. It was a pressure job in which I was never fully in control."

Unlike Crocus Hill, Cottingwood is a success. Besides her partner and boyfriend, John Foley, who is one of the two cooks, she employs several full- and part-time workers. Karen is expanding the catering operation, which now accounts for over one-third of sales by staging theme parties, Sunday brunches, and other special gourmet events in keeping with the lifestyle of the Cottingwood neighborhood.

Karen works 80 hours a week, longer hours than she did as a Pinstripe Petite executive. There is a difference, however. "There is an absence of corporate accountability. If you want to make a change in the store's decor, there is no need for a slide presentation and a proposal. You just go ahead and do it."

Closing Crocus Hill and buying a second store has also changed her lifestyle. When she moved to St. Paul, Karen bought a home and a classic Mercedes-Benz. The home is on the market, and Karen and John now live in the apartment over the store.

Selling Yachts on Long Island Sound

Grove Ely (late fifties) is a niche marketer, and his vehicle, R. J. Ely & Sons, sells and services inboard motorboats and yachts and operates a 250-boat marina in Rowayton, Connecticut.

More than a business, R. J. Ely & Sons represents Ely's personal philosophy of "grow or die." At 35, he walked away from a corporate marketing job at the Shulton Company. After attending the University of Pennsylvania Wharton School of Finance and a brief training program at an advertising agency, he worked 10 years for Chesebrough-Pond's, Inc.

"I changed jobs, and for three years and eight months I commuted 59 miles each way from Connecticut to Shulton in Clifton, New Jersey. In the process, I wore out a Mercedes-Benz. By then, I didn't believe that I could stand writing another marketing plan for a deodorant, aftershave, or face cream. I was well paid but there was no joy here."

Ely's star must have risen in the heavens when his wife heard that a local boatyard was for sale. Knowing his interest in boats, she asked him if he planned to buy it. Ely was soon saying goodbye to Shulton and a salary that was not too easy to replace in a boatyard business.

"It was shocking how little I knew about the business even though I have been around boats since I was a youngster."

Until then, sailing had been a hobby. He soon learned that the ability to prepare marketing plans and sell products carries over from one field to another, even those as different as male toiletries and boats. In both fields you need to understand what customers want, but how you gather information in each field differs. In packaged goods he relied on formalized market research studies, and in the boat business he listens personally to customers.

Over the past 20 years, the Rowayton boatyard has changed market directions several times to keep pace with business conditions and market trends. The company no longer builds boats. It switched to being a sales agent for several lines of yachts, a maintenance and service business, and the operator of one of Long Island Sound's larger marinas.

"If anything, I live by the phrase 'grow or die.' When you get up in the morning you have to plan your life in a way that lets you grow. Don't go thinking, 'I'm going to hold on to what I have.' Because what you hold onto gradually diminishes. If you don't seek new horizons, you disappear."

This Retailer Skis on Wednesday Afternoons

Nearly one-half of Patrick Monroe's (early fifties) life has been spent in consumer product sales and corporate marketing. Little did he realize that what he learned over a 25-year period at Pillsbury Company, American Home Products, Colgate-Palmolive Company, Lever Brothers Company (American District Telegraph Company), and his last job as general manager of London Rubber Company would ever be applicable in his own business.

Ever since he graduated from college in the early 1960s, Pat worked in sales or marketing jobs. During his corporate climb, he watched as talented executives were fired or lulled into false security by corporate benefits. These experiences readied him for change. "After a while, I thought that there was more to life than climbing the ladder. As you make more money, you spend even more. But you're never in control. You become a victim of a company's 'golden handcuffs.' "

Pat was joined in considering a different career by his wife, Joyce, an apparel designer and retailer. Both Monroes are big-city products: Pat from Detroit and Joyce from New York City. To meet their objectives of self-employment and living in a smaller community, they moved to Manchester Center, Vermont. They purchased Wilson's Country Clothes and settled into the lifestyle of rural Vermont. "I don't have time for long vacations, but I can at least take off a Wednesday afternoon and go skiing."

The Monroes sold their Ridgewood, New Jersey home in 1986 at the peak of the real estate boom. They invested about $100,000 of the profits in Wilson's and used the balance to buy a larger home in Vermont. Mortgage and taxes together were still considerably less than their previous mortgage payments.

Even with their careful market planning, Wilson's was not a success. No sooner than Pat moved to Manchester Center, a village with a year-round population of only 3500, than the area became even more of a shopping meca, with nearly 75 discount fashion outlet stores, including Calvin Klein, Ltd., Ralph Lauren Corporation and Brooks Brothers. Their presence, along with a slowdown in the local economy, depressed Wilson's sales and profits.

Pat considered business alternatives that were less dependent on tourists, skiers, and fashion trends. Using his corporate marketing skills to analyze different businesses, he started Village Valet, a dry-cleaning and repair service. He visited and talked with dry cleaners in other communities, he analyzed profit-and-loss statements available from trade associations, and he learned how to operate the equipment.

Based on his study, he wrote a 30-page business plan based on a concept to broaden Village Valet from a traditional dry cleaner to one that offers laundry, shoe repair, weaving, and tuxedo rental, services easily taken for granted in suburban New Jesey but not as accessible to the residents of Manchester Center.

Once established, Pat closed Wilson's and rented the store at a profit. Joyce became the manager of a retail outlet in Manchester Center. A year later, Village Valet is meeting its sales objectives even though Pat's salary is far below his corporate earnings.

CAREER OPPORTUNITIES IN BOOKSELLING

If the statistics are any indication, the nation's booksellers seem to be thriving. The number of bookstores have grown 76 percent since 1980, to over 17,000, and during the five-year period from 1986 to 1991, notes the American Booksellers Association, the growth in retail sales was equally impressive, rising from $4.9 to $7.9 billion. Booksellers attribute this growth to a demand for general, nonfiction, children's, travel, and reference books and to novels that appeal to adult readers.

Even with the book chains penetrating the marketplace and the availability of books in nontraditional retail outlets, independents have maintained a strong market share and in many communities are the dominant vendors. The two largest book retailers in the United States, both independents, are located in Denver and Portland, Oregon.

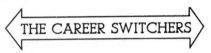

A Wall Street Broker Turns to Books

A peripatetic life as a youngster is perhaps one of the secrets behind the steady growth of Northshire Books in Manchester Center, Vermont. Edward Morrow, Jr. (midfifties) spent the equivalent of his junior high school years in France. He went to high school in Argentina while his namesake father covered post-World War II and the Perón government for the *New York Times*.

Ed left Middlebury College in Vermont after his second year and served several years with the merchant marine. After returning home, he graduated from Columbia University and with a continuing interest in third world countries, Ed joined CARE and spent six years overseas.

"By this time, I was married, in my late twenties and our two sons had been born. I wanted the boys to have permanent roots during their school years. Washington would have been the natural place to work, but I did not want a bureaucratic office job."

Instead he joined and became a partner in a small Wall Street firm, but he soon became dissatisfied with the business. "I decided to look for something different, preferably my own business in which my wife would be my partner."

Other than knowing they wanted to move to New England, the Morrows were open to suggestions. Using newspaper classified ads as a starter, they looked at restaurants, inns, bookstores, and even a sawmill in northern Vermont.

They visited different communities, investigated a number of fields, spoke to merchants, and evaluated different businesses, eventually narrowing the field to bookselling. The clincher came when Ed attended a five-day orientation seminar conducted by the American Booksellers Association for prospective buyers. Little did he realize that he would be president of this association 15 years later.

He continued to work in Wall Street as he evaluated possible store sites. It took two years to find a location that met their needs: a good place to live and an area that could support a bookstore. Barbara wanted to buy an existing bookstore with a proven record. Although Barbara's approach seemed like a safer option, Ed preferred starting their own store and building the business their way.

to speed on what we wanted in a store, and we were confident that the area could support a quality bookstore." (See Pat Monroe's profile earlier in this chapter.)

By the mid-1980s Northshire Books had grown beyond the Morrow's initial forecasts. By now they had divided the responsibilities for running the store: Barbara is the book buyer and Ed the general manager. A priority was more space. They bought and renovated a former inn with 8700 square feet. The space is large enough to stock 33,000 different titles, the depth Ed considers necessary to satisfy a diverse customer base of local and second-home residents, day-trippers, and winter and summer tourists.

"We're a magnet store, drawing well beyond our market area. It's still a struggle, but we run a profitable business that employs over 30 people."

An Omnivorous Collector Becomes a Book Dealer

When Richard Weiner (early forties) was a Colgate University student, he seemed destined for a career as a lawyer. Before entering the University of Pennsylvania Law School, Dick continued his French studies at Harvard University, followed by two years in the U.S. Navy.

After graduating from law school, Dick clerked for two years for a Federal District Court judge in Philadelphia and spent several years in New Jersey as an assistant attorney general working on child abuse cases. While at law school, Dick visited Philadelphia auction galleries and started a book collection. As with many inveterate collectors, his collection grew.

About 1980, while Dick was still working for the attorney general's office, his girlfriend, now his wife, suggested that he find outside space for what had become a rather large collection. Dick opened Escargot Books, a specialty store dealing in used and collector books, in Brielle, an upper-income community on the New Jersey shore. Two years later Dick gave up the law to concentrate on collecting and selling.

What doesn't show in Dick's biography are the range of courses he took at Colgate. "I had a smorgasbord education. I majored in French, and as a minor, I took introductory courses at random from astronomy to philosophy. Little did I know then how useful this assorted knowledge would be in evaluating and selecting books."

Owns the Largest African-American Bookstore

Like Ed Morrow and Richard Weiner, Clara Villarosa (early sixties) also learned bookselling on the job. Clara is the founder, president, and principal shareholder in Denver's Hue-Man Experience Bookstore, which sells the largest collection of African-American literature in the Rocky Mountain region, if not the nation.

Clara started the Hue-Man Experience, a play on words for "man of color," in 1984 to sell books that are by, about, and of special interest to African-Americans. It was meant to fill the cultural void for Denver's 100,000 blacks, which was created when the city's only other minority-owned bookstore closed several years earlier.

No newcomer to career changing, Clara arrived in Denver in 1968 and for the next 12 years held a series of jobs at Children's Hospital as chief of psychiatric social work, director of the department of behavioral sciences, and assistant hospital administrator.

She left the hospital in 1980 to earn a doctorate in social work from Denver University. To pay college expenses, Clara worked as a human resource officer for a local bank. She was also formulating plans for a business, and before she even completed her degree, the entrepreneurial urge got the better of her.

She started Hue-Man Experience, not so much to fulfill a lifelong business dream but, like so many career changers, to be in charge. She wanted to serve and enrich Denver's African-American community. "As I explored different possibilities, it was obvious that Denver lacked a bookstore just for us."

"What did I know about bookselling? Very little. I guess I had lots of chutzpah (nerve), help from two partners who have since left, $35,000 in seed money, and the support of my store's board of directors. I learned about retailing by questioning customers and other booksellers, working 10 hours a day, and attending workshops for owners of small businesses." Once a social worker, always a social worker, and in social work Clara discovered how to deal with different types of people, from children to adults, and to interpret their needs.

The Hue-Man Experience stocks about 3000 books and sells a line of prints, carvings, and jewelry, all reflective of Clara's social philosophy. Within the next few years, she plans to launch a national mail-order business. After fighting for survival, the Hue-Man Experience has sales of $250,000 and Clara now earns about half of her former bank salary.

CAREER OPPORTUNITIES IN
BED-AND-BREAKFAST INNS

Market estimates vary, but they show that there are approximately 12,000 to 15,000 U.S. inns with 4 to 24 rooms. Over a 10-year period spanning the 1980s, the number of inns increased over 200 percent. Differentials in market statistics notwithstanding, B&Bs have indeed grown in popularity. Little wonder that B&Bs attract so many would-be career changers.

Some potential buyers have a quixotic notion that running an inn would be a "fun" business, requiring little work or even absentee ownership. If these are the prime motivations, forget it. Even if you enjoy being a B&B guest, is this a reason to buy an inn?

There are, however, sound business reasons for the popularity of inns. Most notably, they provide ambiance, individualism, and a personal touch, qualities not normally found in most chain-operated hotels and motels. The proprietor needs to be somewhat of a master of ceremonies, being highly visible, welcoming guests, talking with them, and making them feel like family.

Owning a B&B, whether it is year-round or seasonal, counters any concept of a semiretirement lifestyle; there's little relaxation when catering to vacationers and travelers.

B&Bs are basically real estate investments. The secret is to know when to sell the inn at a profit.

Many of the answers of inn management can be found in a wealth of books, reference guides, and newsletters or by attending how-to seminars on innkeeping.

THE CAREER SWITCHERS

On-the-Job Training in Inn Management

Barry Rein (early fifties) is a corporate manager, honed by over 20 years of experience as a chemist and then as a marketer of chemical products. A chemistry major at Pennsylvania State University, Barry also has an MBA and worked first as a chemist and then a manager for a number of chemical companies.

During his executive climb, he and his wife, Cathy, a lawyer and executive vice president at Metropolitan Life Insurance Company, bought a home in Cape May, New Jersey, a resort community at the southern tip of the state. In the early 1980s, the Continental Group, Inc., his employer at the time, was sold and Barry executed his golden parachute contract.

Barry considered buying or starting a specialty chemical company, but instead he used the proceeds to buy a dilapidated, turn-of-the-century Victorian home with the intention of converting it into a seasonal bed-and-breakfast inn.

His timing was perfect. Several hundred Cape May homes were being restored as private residences or inns and given landmark status.

The Reins completely gutted the three-story building and furnished its 20 rooms with authentic Victorian fixtures. Barry was a novice. His knowledge of antiques was scant, and he knew even less about restoring and operating a B&B. He knew how to develop five-year corporate plans and use computerized Project Evaluation and Review Technique charts, but he had never done this type of planning before.

It took nearly two years to ready Columns-by-the-Sea for its first guest, but it didn't take too long to learn that running a B&B is hard work.

"Even when you have a staff, there comes a time when you personally must clean bathroom floors and make beds. If you think this is beneath your dignity, then inn ownership is not for you. We learned about running a B&B by doing it."

When the renovation started on the inn, Barry's original intention was to hire a manager to run it on a day-to-day basis, but he soon found that he enjoyed the personal involvement. "It's time to sell when the work is no longer fun."

A Different B&B Formula

In contrast to Columns-by-the-Sea, which operates on a eight-month season in a resort community, Penni Johnson (midforties) and Susan Moehl (midthirties) opened the Southmoreland as a year-round urban inn in downtown Kansas City, Missouri.

Like Barry Rein, Penni and Susan also left high-profile corporate and professional positions to create an urban inn that was designed for both vacationing and corporate travelers. Most inns are located in resort or rural areas, but Southmoreland is a trend-setter as the only inn bordering on Kansas City's premier inner city shopping center.

"We wanted to buy an inn in Maine, but property was too costly and only seasonal. The inn, above all, had to produce a healthy

Kansas City. There were many large hotels in the area, but our inn would be unique."

Southmoreland opened in July 1990 based on the principles outlined in its 75-page mission statement and business plan. Recognizing that both Penni and Susan were career switchers, they incorporated the business under the name White-Collar Dropouts. It took a year to virtually raze the 1913 mansion, bring it up to commercial code, and add 6000 square feet, a veranda, a parking lot, and a carriage house to serve as Penni and Susan's home.

During this transition period, Penni, a lawyer and educator, continued working as a college administrator, and Susan, who has an MBA from Northwestern University, left her Hallmark Cards, Inc. marketing job to supervise the project. Construction was handled by professionals, but the two owners researched and decorated each of the 12 bedrooms in authentic period furnishings. They named the rooms in honor of past Kansas City celebrities, such as baseball player Satchel Paige and artist Thomas Hart Benton, and furnished them appropriately.

As former corporate executives, they have included amenities expected by corporate travelers: fax service and modem connections for desktop and portable computers. This investment paid off: over 25 percent of their revenues, more than their initial forecast, are generated from the corporate community.

Their approach to inn management has already been recognized by rating groups. Within a year of Southmoreland's opening, it was cited in several "best 10" lists.

From the first day, they realized that owning a successful B&B requires a dedication to service that differs from that required for other service-oriented businesses.

"You have to know how to read your customers. Some customers look at you as servants; others respect you as entrepreneurs. But you are still running a service business, and in our case, other than some part-time workers, we do everything ourselves, beginning at 5 in the morning when breakfast baking starts."

CAREER OPPORTUNITIES AS A COOK AND RESTAURANTEUR

One way to learn how to cook professionally is to take a professional cooking course. Others pick up skills as an apprentice or convert a hobby into a full-time career. Many cooks also own restaurants, and then the cook's creativity must blend with the practicalities of running a retail business.

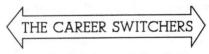

THE CAREER SWITCHERS

A Lawyer Runs One of New York's Best

After Barry Wine (late forties) graduated from the University of Chicago Law School, his career path looked certain. He was hired by a "white shoe" law firm, Breed Abbott Morgan. He stayed there only two years: not that he was dissatisfied with the life of a Wall Street corporate lawyer, but he wanted to work and live outside New York City.

Barry moved to New Paltz, in the Hudson River Valley, 75 miles north of New York City, to practice law as a solo practitioner. The town, with its Hugenot and Victorian architecture, had a 1960s cachet (it's only a few miles from Woodstock). As a small town lawyer with little income, he and his wife, Susan, and their two children, lived in an apartment over his ground floor law office.

Five years later, Barry, now with an established practice, bought several Victorian homes on Academy Street, one of New Paltz's main shopping streets. Susan opened an art shop and a dress store, and as a business proposition, Barry thought it made sense to use part of one building as a restaurant. "If nothing more, we could run fashion shows in conjunction with lunch."

Operating a restaurant was realistic to a working lawyer because a source of cooks was readily available through the Culinary Institute of America, situated directly across the Hudson in Hyde Park. "I made an arrangement with a CIA instructor to cook and run the business. At the last moment, he got cold feet. Since I had a liquor license, I decided to get involved. At the time, I knew nothing about the restaurant business, nor was I a cook."

Other CIA-trained chefs proved to be unsatisfactory. Some failed to show up for work and others were not up to his standards. The restaurant, originally called Maxine's, was open only on Friday and Saturday nights. During the week, Barry practiced law. As a result of some favorable newspaper reviews, Maxine's attracted customers, and it was renamed the Quilted Giraffe.

What was once a part-time venture and hobby changed in 1977, when Barry became a full-time restauranteur. By New Paltz standards prices were high, but its menu and decor appealed to customers. "We were coming to New York City to buy provisions, and with our children about to start school, it seemed like a good time to move back to New York."

Replying to a restaurant for sale ad in the *New York Times,* Barry bought and remodeled what was the Bonanza Coffee Shop on Second Avenue and 51st Street, around the corner from Lutece, then as now one of New York's premiere restaurants. Several years later he moved the Quilted Giraffe to its present Madison Avenue location.

Barry, who has never taken a formal cooking lesson, learned to cook by reading, practicing, and visiting many of France's three- and four-star restaurants.

Several trips to Japan inspired him to introduce New York diners to a version of the *Kaiseki Kyoto* dinner, a nine-course meal, served on appropriate porcelain and lacquer dinnerware and eaten with chopsticks. It is priced at $135, nearly 50 percent higher than the regular fixed-price dinner. To prepare and serve such a dinner requires the type of staff communications that Wine says are unique to fine New York restaurants.

Barry has not practiced law for nearly 15 years, but he's never been able to shake his legal training. "We run the Quilted Giraffe based on the Socratic method of teaching, which I learned in law school. It teaches the staff to think independently and creatively. We couldn't serve Kaiseki dinners if we didn't have this discipline and the ability to communicate."

What's Tastier: PR or Cooking?

If it weren't for a trip that Elaine Knechtel (midthirties) took to Italy in 1989, she most likely would still be working full-time as a publicist. The trip came at a time in her professional life when she was puzzled about the direction of her career. "What are my real skills? What can I really do? I found no answer."

Ever since she graduated from the University of California– Berkeley, Elaine went up the ladder as a publicist. Like many recent college graduates who like to write, it was only natural for her to find employment as a publicist.

For the next 10 years, Elaine worked for several high-tech companies and public relations firms, including Regis McKenna, Inc. then in its glory days as the PR agency for some of the nation's fastest growing computer companies. Within five years, she was earning in the mid-$50,000s and was an account supervisor.

"I never felt professionally and personally satisfied with the work. I knew it was the essence of the service business to stay behind the scenes, but I wanted more from work than to make others look good. At the same time I was questioning my work, I took a three-week vacation to Italy. I saw people really enjoying their work. Perhaps it was the 'grass is always greener' story once again, but I returned from Italy, quit my job, yet had little idea of what I was going to do."

Because she was single, Elaine only had to reduce her personal expenses. During this transition period, she took classes in Italian and painting, read a lot, and planned her next move. To meet expenses, she started a public relations consultancy in her home with the idea that she would work part-time and spend the balance of the time evaluating new career alternatives.

To her own surprise, in her first nine months in business, Elaine made more money than she would have earned at Regis McKenna. What helped during her transition was an informal support group she had formed with other career changers. The group met regularly and served as an ad hoc outplacement service.

"During this period, one factor remained constant. I was cooking. I always liked to cook but I never thought of it as a career. But I soon found the enthusiasm for cooking that I lacked in public relations. Unlike the PR business, I could talk about food, brag about it, and be proud of my work."

It seemed apparent that cooking would become the focus of her new life. San Francisco, where she lived, had a selection of cooking schools geared to training professionals. After completing a three-month course in classic French cooking, Elaine had to modify her personal objectives to make a living.

She caters, gives private cooking lessons, and works part-time for a new public relations firm that was recently started by two former Regis McKenna employees. Both are mothers with young children who need flextime to balance children, home, and work. Elaine manages some of the accounts in their absence.

"In making the changeover to cooking, I learned that I no longer have to live in an either-or world. Until my cooking business is self-sufficient, I can straddle two work environments—cooking and public relations—and enjoy them both."

Hollywood's Producer of Designer Doughnuts

Dennis Hoffman (early fifties) is a lifelong Los Angeles resident, and for more than 30 of these years, his career has been linked with Hollywood. When Hoffman was ready to make a career change in 1988, his selection had a show business flair.

He created Designer Donuts on a whim and opened a bakery on Sunset Boulevard in Hollywood to bake and sell "trendy" donuts to film and TV studios. It is an industry tradition to give complimentary donuts to everyone working on a film set. Designer Donuts is set up to meet that demand even when it means delivering up to 14,000 donuts in 48 hours.

Dennis' film production career is also classic Hollywood: Universal Studios as a film splicer after graduating from high school, followed by nine years learning the nuances of titles and special effects at another studio.

At 29, he founded his own titles company, Cinfx. The company did well, and a few years later it was bought by Filmways, then a high-roller TV production company. A few years later, Filmways had financial troubles, and Dennis and his partners bought back the company.

"About this time, I was introduced to Steven Spielberg, a 19-year-old student at Long Beach State College who needed money to produce a 20-minute film. I put it up, and *Amber*, which he directed, won the Atlanta Film Festival award.

As part of our contractual agreement, I had the option to participate with Spielberg in any film of my choice. Spielberg by then had become a hot new Hollywood name, and he bought out my contract, along with the name *Amber*."

After Cinfx was acquired for the second time, Hoffman started another title company. He might have stayed in the title business indefinitely, but the emerging technology of videotaping made obsolete certain aspects of TV filming, to the point that Dennis and his financial supporters closed the company.

What do you do when you're nearing 50 and your entire life has focused on a single industry? Make a 180-degree career change, or as Dennis decided, take advantage of your industry know-how. As with so many ventures, Dennis, the entrepreneur, started with a simple concept. He knew that bland donuts were the usual breakfast fare at most production studios.

"When I started Designer Donuts, I knew nothing about baking. My education consisted of an equipment supplier's two-day workshop. But I knew Hollywood, how the studios think, how they buy, and who does the buying.

"Donuts differ from special effects. Hardly a high-ticket item, they are bought solely on price. It's a nickel-and-dime business. We changed their thinking by making our donuts different and by giving them exotic names—Dutch apple crunch, raspberry rage, luscious lemon, and peanut butter and jelly."

———————◆———————

Points to Remember

► Most retailers learn their business on the job.
► There is a high mortality rate.
► Hard work is one of the keys to success.
► There's always room for a new niche retailer.
► Specialty independent bookstores do well.
► Owning a bed-and-breakfast is not for an absentee owner.
► B&Bs can make good real estate investments.

———————◆———————

CHAPTER 15

Home Improvement and Decor

CAREER OPPORTUNITIES

Home decor, as defined in *It's Never Too Late*, is pursued by craftspeople and entrepreneurs whose work relates to the home. These career changers acquired and perfected their skills on the job. Because they are in a service business, they approached their new careers like many of the people profiled in Chapter 14.

THE CAREER SWITCHERS

Keeping Your Chimneys Clean

David Eakin (midforties), a teacher turned chimney sweep, continues to use his teaching skills every day in serving northern New Jersey home owners.

By the time David was in his midthirties, he had taught high school English for over 10 years. Like many teachers, he needed supplemental income to support his family, and his cousin suggested he work part-time for him as a chimney sweep.

It was a growth period for chimney sweeps as several factors produced a late 1970s resurgence in fireplace use. Home owners were reacting to several Middle East oil crises and subsequent price rises in heating oil. Environmentalists were advocating the use of wood over fossil fuel in heating homes.

It seemed like an ideal situation. He could continue teaching and, after school and on weekends, learn a new trade and earn extra money. In a little over a year, David left teaching. He enjoyed the freedom of working on his own. Being a chimney sweep also seemed like a good way to avoid the common problem of teacher burnout.

Before establishing the Village Sweep, David promoted his service to attract customers. He also attended a workshop on chimney sweeping. Wearing the sweep's classic coat and tails and top hat and adhering to the image characterized in *Mary Poppins*, are hardly the credentials necessary to build a business, however. Fortunately, he learned this important lesson at the outset of his new career.

The Village Sweep, now grown to include several employees and two vans, serves the needs of a cluster of suburban New Jersey communities. In managing the Village Sweep, David has applied a number of skills borrowed from the classroom.

"Teachers like to talk. I'm no exception. We also like to explain, and I spend a good part of my time communicating the safety values of a clean chimney."

Then there is David's quest for organization, a quality also inherited from the classroom. He computerized his records and customer mailing list in 1984, several years before most smaller businesses began to automate.

As a teacher, David was the adviser to the schools' newspaper, an experience that helps in the desktop publishing of a promotional newsletter that he mails several times a year to 5000 customers.

A Career Changer Trains Paperhangers

By training and work experience, Jeffrey Keelan (late thirties) hardly qualifies as a career counselor. In addition to technically preparing students to be wallpaperers, as the founder and director of the Paper Hanging Institute, he counsels many students who are making the transition from office and management jobs to craft work.

After graduating from the University of Hartford as a marketing major, Jeff worked for nearly 10 years as a department store buyer and a sales representative for a men's sportswear manufacturer. "Although I became the company's top salesman in the country, I wanted to run my own business. There's really no security in working for someone else."

While studying a number of fields, he learned about opportunities as a paperhanger, the shortage of skilled craftspeople in the field, and the low capital investment needed to get into business. These were critical factors, since his financial resources were limited.

He lacked formal training, so Jeff became an apprentice for several months before launching his own papering business. Once established, Jeff, the former salesman, divided his time between hanging paper and marketing his services.

When Keelan Paper Hanging attracted a number of papering job and Jeff had two to three months of backlogged work, he was asked by customers and craftspeople in other fields how they could get into a field that was then paying over $300 a day. These inquiries encouraged Jeff to establish the Paper Hanging Institute in 1987, one of only four or five accredited schools in the United States dedicated to the wallpapering trade.

The school has already trained several hundred students in an intensive 400-hour program over a 10-week period, which costs about $2800. There's more to the school's program than learning the fine points of papering.

Jeff helps students organize their businesses and advises them on how to sell their services effectively. Students include former bank vice presidents, corporate executives, accountants and police, and Jeff guides them in making the successful transition to a new lifestyle as craftspeople.

"We teach more than hands-on skills. It's important that students develop a positive 'craft attitude.' They need to feel proud that they own their businesses. I emphasize the advantages of independence and self-employment. For many students, it is the first time in their business lives that they don't have to worry that a younger, better educated person has just moved into the next office and wants their job."

Wall Street Administrator Becomes a Jeff Keelan Disciple

Nancy Wickstrom (early thirties) is a Jeff Keelan fan. In her prewallpapering days, Nancy promised that she'd leave Wall Street just as soon as she received her next annual bonus. She renewed that promise each year.

Nancy had worked for Goldman Sachs & Company for more than nine years, where she managed the firm's daily cash flow. Like so many middle managers, she was trapped by the "golden handcuffs" of a comfortable corporate environment and a lifestyle that is difficult to discard when you're earning over $90,000 a year. The good life aside, Nancy was getting itchy to do something different.

Her ambivalence ended in mid-1989 when she was laid off, one of thousands to be eliminated as Wall Street investment firms drastically cut administrative and professional staffs. Unlike many of her associates, Nancy was single, debt free and thrifty, and had already saved more than $100,000 is an IRA and a 401(k) plan.

Before she was ready to tackle a new job, she traveled for two months and considered a number of different careers. An outplacement consultant, discovering her interest in art and photography, suggested that she look at crafts.

She had little difficulty making the changeover to blue-collar work. Her father is a retired carpenter, and her two brothers are plumbers. Nancy's long-standing interest in art influenced her decision. The actual clincher to become a paperer was seeing Jeff Keelan being interviewed on TV.

Taking a craft course is one matter; earning a living as a professional represents a different set of challenges. Nancy, however, realized that as a paperer she would have a decided edge: many people paint their homes, but they rarely paper them. Only one year after Goldman Sachs and completion of her training, she went into business for herself.

"I had to get customers and learn more about papering. The best way is to work with house painters who don't paper. I took a job two days a week at a paint store to meet contractors, learn more about materials, and get referrals.

Being a woman has some definite advantages. Most decorating decisions are made by women, and they appear more comfortable talking to me than to male paperers. When I work for them they feel less threatened about having me in the house."

He Builds Custom Furniture

Little did Murray Hulse (late fifties) realize that his father's indifference to do-it-yourself work would be his initial introduction to handicrafts. As a teenager, his father relegated home repairs to Murray but also encouraged his skills with gifts of woodworking equipment.

"At Hamilton College, I started out in premed but switched into a dual music and biology major, literally teaching frogs how to sing." For 18 years, Murray worked in sales and management positions at several Aetna Life & Casualty branch offices in Michigan. In the mid-1970s, he changed companies.

He relocated to Boston and started selling employee benefit plans. Over the next 16 years, Murray redefined his career even more as he moved from selling to consulting.

His bubble burst in 1990 when he lost his job. This wasn't the first time that Murray considered severing his ties with the insurance industry. Only a few years earlier in 1988, while still an employee benefits consultant, he and his wife, Dory, as an experiment, started a mail-order company to build and sell small cabinets.

Murray used his marketing skills and Dory, who worked for an advertising agency at the time, created and placed ads in the *New Yorker* and *Colonial Homes* magazines. The response was good, but Murray was not ready to give up his job and move on a full-time basis into the mail-order business.

He actually preferred designing and making custom furniture and working directly with customers. "From the time I got married, I was building furniture for the home. Dining room. Living room. Children's furniture. And when there were ups and downs in business, I found woodworking excellent therapy."

When he lost his job, Murray was assigned to an outplacement firm. Career options started to gel when Murray decided it was time to work for himself. His outplacement counselor taught him how to plan the move, think through each step, and pursue a course of action. Most importantly, Murray was already a skilled and confident craftsman.

He started Time & Again Furnishings in 1990 to build and restore custom furniture and cabinetry. Ridgewood, New Jersey, where the Hulses live, is an upscale suburban community where residents can afford quality furniture.

"There's an advantage in living in Ridgewood and knowing the people. From my years in selling insurance, I know how to present myself. And, unlike some craftsmen, I don't resent wearing a shirt and tie and putting on airs to get a sale."

This is not to say that Murray finds furniture building an easy way to make a living. His wife has a full-time job that provides a financial cushion and covers fringe benefits. During 1991, Time & Again met its business plan. It also moved out of his basement to a different location, and Murray has hired a full-time carpenter.

She Markets Kitchen Accessories

Beverly Margolis (late fifties) is proud of her different careers, including the last few, which focus on the kitchen and cooking, which gave her the experience and confidence to launch what is now a multi-million dollar merchandising company.

Her cooking career actually began when she was very young, when her mother was a kosher caterer in Buffalo. When Beverly was 16, she attended a Le Cordon Bleu course in France, the start of a lifelong interest in cooking.

After graduating from college, Beverly traveled the expected route for women of that day: she taught school, got married, had children, and then went back to teaching. She was also a gourmet cooking instructor, proprietor of a cooking school affiliated with a Utica, New York supermarket, and the hostess of a public television cooking program.

When Beverly was 49, she became an entrepreneur, a business move she never planned. The concept germinated when she and her husband bought a condominium in Florida. The kitchen was inadequately supplied with acceptable housewares, so she asked a number of Florida builders and developers about this deficiency. The answer was always the same. Nobody was interested in prestocking a kitchen with dishes, glasses, and utensils. She returned to Utica, and Beverly Pac, Ltd. was born in 1981.

"As you would expect, it was trial and error from the start. As a cook, I of course knew from first-hand experience what products are needed in a kitchen. Fortunately I had assistance. My father, then in his late eighties, helped me with inventory scheduling and showed me how to warehouse goods, and my husband, who is a dentist and a computer expert, insisted that we computerize all parts of the business, an important factor when you run a warehouse operation."

As Beverly Pac was being launched, it was fortunately supported by a parallel trend in hotel and motel room design. In an effort to attract a greater market share of business travelers, vacationers, and retirees, two-room suites with kitchens were replacing the traditional one-room bedroom units.

This helped to establish Beverly Pac's niche strategy of selling new and replacement kitchen accessories and linens in bulk to hotels, motels, time-sharing resorts, and condominiums. She also created product lines to qualify Beverly Pac as a supplier of home goods to support disaster relief and homeless family programs.

No sooner had Beverly Pac gained market acceptance than its own survival was at stake. Water used in putting out another tenant's fire flooded the Beverly Pac warehouse located in the floor below. It destroyed much of Beverly Pac's inventory; Beverly and her family invested more money. Sales staggered while the warehouse was being rebuilt and restocked, but Beverly Pac was fortunately protected since it had no direct competitors ready to step in and capture its market share.

One of the irreplaceable casualties of the flood was the book that Beverly has yet to finish, *Some Women Are Risk Takers*.

Preparing for a Career in Interior Design

Commuting from suburban New Jersey to New York City and her job as an administrator in a Wall Street commodity firm sapped Catherine Cichowski's (early forties) energy.

The commute was made even more tedious after her daughter was born. She was reluctant, however, to leave her job since the bonus alone exceeded her husband's salary as teacher. In a scenario all too familiar in late twentieth century living, a second salary was necessary to support the family's lifestyle.

Like so many other commuters, Cathy believed her solution would be a job nearer to home and her young daughter. Her transition started in real estate sales, a natural career choice since the suburban New Jersey home and commercial market was booming.

Even so, the irregular work schedule countered Cathy's lifestyle and employment goals. She reasoned that it was time to find a more permanent career.

Where were the best opportunites? Cathy had worked in a number of sales-related jobs. She found that each new job built on the previous. Skills learned on Wall Street increased her poise and confidence; five years in market research with a pharmaceutical company taught her the ABC's of selling. This potpourri of skills came together in interior design, a field in which she could work from home and at the same time satisfy her creative needs.

Cameo Interior Design, which handles home and commercial interiors, operates from a 12 by 20 foot, at-home office. "I was looking for flexibility, and I got it. I start my work day as early at 5:30, but by working from home I can take a few minutes off each morning to walk my daughter to the school bus.

"I've learned some valuable lessons. I was naive about the cost of going into business, the need to operate on a lean budget and to keep overhead costs low. Without an advertising budget, I became a joiner. It's a good way to give out cards and meet people."

------------◆------------

Points to Remember

► There are entrepreneurial opportunites for self-starters.

► Niche home decor and craft fields abound.

► Some career changers must make a psychological adjustment in going from management jobs to blue-collar work.

► Previous skills in the field are not mandatory.

► Skills can be learned on the job.

► There are opportunites to work at home or nearby.

------------◆------------

CHAPTER 16

Gardening, Farming, and the Environment

CAREER OPPORTUNITIES IN GARDENING

It's one thing to be a weekend gardener, still another to make a living as a horticulturist. No longer a field for amateurs, today's professionals must know the science of botany, tree maintenance, plant propagation, and physiology and are trained to function under rigid environmental conditions.

Most modern-day horticulturists have attended community and four-year colleges or equivalency programs conducted by such institutions as Longwood Gardens (suburban Philadelphia) and the New York Botanical Gardens.

Jobs range from those at botanical gardens, arboretums, and government agencies to entrepreneurial opportunities in service and product companies serving this multibillion dollar industry.

Career changers should be aware that entry-level jobs require manual skills. If horticulture is for you—get in shape.

THE CAREER SWITCHERS

The Fashion Designer Turns Gardener

Changing careers is nothing new to Jane Brook Barba (midforties). Jane has been a cofounder of a natural food cooperative, a realtor, a designer of children's clothes, and a horticulturist. Throughout her diverse career, much of her work has been related to the environment.

Jane was a gardener by the time she was nine. After graduating from high school, she moved to Connecticut and during this period founded a natural food business. After returning to New York, she worked for several years for a realtor and then started a fashion design company, Pure Kid, to design and manufacture children's clothes made exclusively from natural fibers.

"We had some success. One of our customers was Saks Fifth Avenue. The shock came when I figured I was working long hours and earning less than $10 an hour." Jane sold her inventory and mailing list. Now what?

She took a six-week career-counseling course and evaluated various options, including landscape architecture. "I got to asking myself, 'why am I indoors all day when I'm really an outdoors person?' I realized that the esthetics of design are similar in fashion and in gardens. In apparel you work with fabrics, and in gardening with living plants, but in both instances the ability to design is the important element."

Jane had been a gardening hobbyist since childhood, but before turning professional, she completed an 18-month professional certification program at the New York Botanical Gardens. She then found a job with the Council on the Environment, an organization that promotes and develops community gardens in New York City neighborhoods.

As an inveterate entrepreneur, she started American Cottage Gardens, which converts apartment house terraces, penthouses, and townhouse backyards into gardens. Her business is growing and Jane augments her income with a part-time staff job at the New York Botanical Gardens.

A Harvard MBA Selects Horticulture

Josh Huntington's (midforties) entrance into gardening was the opposite of Jane's career switch. Josh is the product of big business, with the education and training expected of a *Fortune* 500 company executive: an engineering degree from Princeton University, a six-year tour in the U.S. Navy as a nuclear engineering officer, a master degree from Catholic University in nuclear engineering, and a Harvard University MBA.

After graduation from Harvard, Josh joined International Paper Company, and over the next 10 years he received prime corporate jobs, including a 3-year overseas assignment as chief financial officer of International Paper's French operating company.

When he returned to the United States, International Paper was in the process of relocating its executive headquarters from New York City to the suburbs. As part of its decentralization plan, Josh's department was transferred to the company's Memphis facility.

As much as he enjoyed working for International Paper, he rejected both the transfer and the new job. He preferred to stay in New York, and with his background in financial management, Josh was hired as a vice president of the First Boston Corporation.

Josh lost his job as First Boston downsized parts of its investment banking operation 30 months later, and he was without an alternative career plan.

Josh always felt at ease in the outdoors, having grown up on a farm in Vermont. He also wanted to break ties with the past. A prime objective was to work in a field in which eventually he could be his own boss. At the same time he was considering an outdoor-related career, he read a newspaper article on the New York Botanical Gardens' educational program. It helped convince him to study horticulture.

"Although horticulture is totally removed from nuclear engineering and corporate financial management, I'm surprised how much I borrow from my past training. As an engineer, I know how to prepare, design, and read contour maps, and as a manager, I see ways to get a job done more efficiently. One thing I know, I'll never make the money I made in industry or on Wall Street, but at least I'll be my own boss."

When Josh, who recently got married, completed the New York Botanical Garden's 18-month course in June 1992, he took the first step in his new career by becoming head gardener on a large suburban New York private estate.

CAREER OPPORTUNITIES IN FARMING

"There's more to being a chicken farmer than attending Chicken U," George Latimer notes later in this chapter. Although all the career changers in *It's Never Too Late* learned about farming and ranching on the job, they could have prepared for a second career by taking agriculture, animal science, and related farm management courses. In addition to owning a farm, some trained farmers manage cooperatives and other farm units.

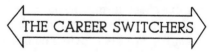
THE CAREER SWITCHERS

Former City Folks Grow Pinot Noir Grapes and Raise Sheep

McMinnville, Oregon, population 19,000 and about 40 miles southwest of Portland, is about 3000 miles from Providence, Rhode Island. To Eve (early forties) and Norman (midfifties) Barnett, operating the 700-acre Youngberg Hill Farm represents a dramatic change of pace.

Both are Easterners. Eve, a professionally trained nurse, taught nursing for a number of years at Northeastern University in Boston, and Norman, who has an MBA and a doctorate from the Harvard University Business School, was a venture capitalist and portfolio manager for more than 20 years.

Although they both had successful careers, they paused to review results and plan a future course. Eve decided to alter the direction of her nursing career by first creating and then directing a learning laboratory for nurses at Northeastern.

Living in Providence, she tired of the two- to three-hour daily commute to Boston. As an alternative, she took the Northeastern formula and established a similar program at the University of Rhode Island School of Nursing.

At the same time that Eve was adjusting her career, Norman left his Boston investment counsel job and founded in Providence the investment firm that bears his name. They're both outdoor people who like to hike, fish, and canoe. New Hampshire was a logical place for a second home, but by the mid-1980s the spread of condominiums and developments meant that they couldn't find suitable property.

"Norman and I realized we were searching for a different lifestyle. We wanted to find an area where we could live, work, and have fun. By our standards, New England was out of the question."

They initially considered opening a U.S.-style inn in Austria, but soon learned that the Austrian government discourages foreigners from making this type of investment. Instead, they looked for property in the United States and found that the Pacific Northwest offered similar lifestyle qualities.

They made seven trips over a one-year period to Oregon, evaluating property and business opportunities before buying the 700-acre Youngberg Hill Farm. Here they created a multipurpose venture consisting of a sheep farm, vineyards for Pinot noir grapes for local wineries, and a five-bedroom inn. Other than scheduled monthly East Coast trips to his Providence office and for client visits, Norman handles most day-to-day investment matters from Oregon.

Youngberg Hill Farm operates as three separate profit centers, with the inn, farm, and vineyard all expected to be profitable. With little formal farm experience, they learned the fundamentals on the job.

At times, they might read a farming manual in the evening and then do the work the following day. Farmers and neighbors are their unofficial teachers, an important factor since the Barnetts run the farm with only one full-time handyman and several part-time workers.

New York City Cop Raises Chickens

When George Latimer (early sixties) returned as deputy chief of the New York City Transit Police in late 1989, the headline in the local civil service newspaper said, "Back in the Saddle Again." From 1977 to mid-1989, George raised chickens on Virginia's eastern shore as a contract farmer for Perdue Farms Inc.

After attending Lincoln University for one year, he worked as a steeplejack and bricklayer. He wanted a more secure job, so he became a subway conductor, and three years later, when he was 25, he joined the transit police.

When George was 37, he was promoted to captain, the youngest officer of that rank in the department's history. George became complacent, a factor eventually leading to his downfall. He started to break away in his early forties, first by learning to ride a motorcycle. He took flying lessons and bought his own airplane.

George, at 47, no longer the department's up-and-comer, was still a captain. Everything seemed to happen at once in 1977. He had just remarried. He retired with half-pay from the transit police and moved to Virginia, where his wife's family lived. George bought a house and became a chicken farmer.

"I wanted a complete change, and I surely got it. I realized the day that I moved to Virginia that it was a mistake. I knew nothing about chicken farming. I even wondered if I would be sent to Chicken U." It was all on-the-job training, with Perdue providing chickens, feed, medicine, and expertise. George raised 60,000 chickens at a time, producing five to six flocks a year.

It was the change of pace that troubled him the most. He ran the farm by himself and did nearly all the work, from feeding the flocks to cleaning three chicken houses between the delivery of new flocks. It didn't take him too long to realize that he missed New York and the more active life of a cop. For excitement, he flew search-and-rescue missions for the U.S. Coast Guard Auxiliary. By the late 1980s, he was ready to move on.

The farm was profitable and he was grossing over $90,000 a year, even though on an hourly basis the pay was low. When Thomas Wolfe said *You Can't Go Home Again*, the warning obviously did not apply to George Latimer. The transit police, with a uniformed force near 4200, had a new chief, an old friend of George's who requested a minority officer at a high policy level.

Although nearly 60 at the time of his appointment as deputy chief, he was welcomed back even after an absence of 11 years.

It took him two years to sell the chicken farm. His wife and some hired workers operated it in his absence. If he learned anything from early retirement, it is the need to have a mature plan; otherwise, don't change.

The Editor Raises Sheep

For 16 years, John Lyons (midforties) worked as a reporter and news editor with two suburban New Jersey daily newspapers, *The Herald–News* and *The Record*.

Within a brief time span, John broke his leg, his father died, and his mother became severely ill. The injury prevented him from working. "I always liked going into New York but on crutches I felt quite vulnerable. I started thinking of moving to a more peaceful area."

John worked in some other fields before becoming a newspaperman. He studied accounting at college to satisfy his CPA father, who wanted him to join his accounting firm. Finance, however, was not to John's liking. As an alternative, he moved to Ireland, did freelance writing, and from his travels in Ireland was introduced to farming and rural living.

While he was attending his mother, he looked for a summer home. Instead he bought an 154-acre dairy farm in the heart of Catskill Mountain dairy country. His avocation turned into a full-time project. He renovated the house and, with little knowledge of sheep farming, bought his first herd.

"I'm from the suburbs, and I knew little about farming. But you can learn a lot from government agencies, cooperative extensions, speaking to other farmers and sheep growers, and reading farming journals."

His immediate goal is to raise enough money from sheep to meet taxes. He is already planning to add beef cattle since they require less attention than sheep and the financial return is better.

John, who is single, operates the farm by himself; a small tractor is the only mechanized equipment that he needs. He thought it would be a more difficult transition from city to rural life, but having worked as a newspaper reporter actually prepared him for the changeover.

He was trained to ask questions, a technique he still finds useful in requesting help from other farmers or talking with government agricultural officials.

Yesterday's Fashion Designer Is Today's Horse Breeder

Growing up in California, Sally Von Wehrlof-Uhlmann (mid-forties) rode horses nearly every day, even qualifying in the fine points of dressage. She quit Antioch College after one year, moved to Spain, and spent several years seeing the world, studying tribal customs, and learning about native food.

By the time that Sally was 24, she married, had a child, moved to Kansas City, Missouri, and started Salaminder, a play on the names of two people who worked with her, Sally and Mindy.

She started Salaminder to do fabric appliqué and soon changed directions to design and manufacture western wear, a move planned to take advantage of the urban cowboy fashion craze of the late 1970s. Salaminder became an industry success story, employing nearly 60 people plus another 14 in sales.

By 1981, the western wear craze slowed down and Salaminder once more changed directions into ladies sportswear. In 1984, Sally, a single parent for 10 years, married Robert Uhlmann, also an entrepreneur and the developer of computer software management systems for broadcast stations. After their son, Lexington, was born, Sally took him regularly to work and even on out-of-town business trips.

Lexington's birth triggered other changes. It forced her to look at the reality of her lifestyle. Sally and her husband bought a ranch 45 minutes south of Kansas City. The property, including a 900-square-foot pre-Civil War building, was completely run-down, with 12-foot weeds and no fencing or workable gates. Although the house had a few redeeming features, Sally renovated it and added a few thousand square feet of additional living space.

"The more time I spent at the ranch, the more I wanted to learn about ranching and return to horses. Here was an opportunity. We started to breed horses, buy livestock, and embark on a program to make the ranch profitable." Life at Salaminder was also becoming even more complex; Sally had too many balls in the air.

Salaminder was sold in early 1990, giving Sally time to devote to building and managing the ranch. As in fashion, where there is a need to anticipate and react quickly to trends, she applies certain fashion industry experience to running the farm. This is as basic as knowing when to repair a machine rather than buy a new one.

CAREER OPPORTUNITIES IN THE ENVIRONMENT

Careers are opening in the enviromental field that hardly existed a generation ago. Law firms hire environmental experts to provide technical know-how to support their legal decisions. Architects and builders are required to prepare detailed environmental impact statements.

To meet these realistic marketplace needs, college curricula are available in environmental engineering, economics, and public administration. Some career changers are also finding business opportunities in niche outdoor specialties, such as environmental consulting and teaching.

THE CAREER SWITCHERS

The Outdoors Through the Eyes of a Camera

"As a teenager in North Carolina, I was the typical consumer, interested mostly in cars, spending money, owning a fur coat, and boys. No sooner than I graduated from high school, I got married. The last thing on my mind was the environment." But since her teenage years in the early 1960s, Helen Longest-Slaughter (mid-forties) has changed her tune.

Helen was a legal secretary in Washington, D.C. for 19 years. When she moved to West Palm Beach, Florida, she found another legal secretarial job. The seeds of change were being sown.

She was disheartened by some of the real estate development clients her employer represented. Disapproving of land development at the expense of Forida's environment, Helen was converted into an active naturalist.

While working at the law firm, she started doing some photography. All she knew about cameras at the time was acquired as a youngster from her father. She increased her photography skills by practicing, reading, and attending workshops. The day of decision arrived. Was she going to continue as an amateur photographer or turn professional?

It wasn't so much that Helen wanted to be a photographer, but she really wanted to do something to help save Florida's environment. "The camera became my way to communicate. I was ready for a gamble. Why not try something new at 40 and fail, rather than wait until you're 70 and never do it."

Helen quit her job as a legal secretary. During the first five years in her new career, she taught nature photography courses through Nature Images, the business she started. The city of West Palm Beach contracted for her services. In teaching photography, the message was the same: "Let the camera tell the story that the land is beautiful and fragile, and that there is reason for its existence."

Helen discovered a more basic problem in the relationship between photography and the environment. Photography magazines advise readers on how to take better pictures, but they miss an important element.

"They ignore nature. They tell readers that they can do just about anything to get a picture, even if in doing so it means disturbing the environment. In my mind, good photography needs to harmonize with nature."

To provide an editorial balance with traditional photography magazines, Helen in mid-1990 along with two partners and several investors launched a bimonthly magazine, *Nature Photography: The Magazine for People Who Love to Photograph Our Natural World*. Even here her legal experience comes in handy.

"I know enough about the law to realize how the magazine can get into trouble and what steps we should take to avoid it."

Living the Dream by Running a Zoo

Between the time I wrote the first and second drafts of *It's Never Too Late*, William Donaldson (then in his early sixties) passed away. His story is unique and deserving of attention in this book. For most of his professional career he was a public administrator, but his lifetime ties to the outdoors helped to create a new career.

Bill Donaldson's professional career took a number of different turns. Only six months before he would have completed training to be an Episcopal priest, he left theology school and embarked on a career that included apprentice embalmer, municipal employee, and city manager of four different cities. In 1979, he became president and chief executive officer of the Zoological Society of Philadelphia, better known as the Philadelphia Zoo.

Throughout his diverse career and back even further as a youngster in rural Colorado, Bill was an avid naturalist and outdoorsman. As a University of Chicago student, he worked part-time at the Chicago Zoo, but much as he liked the work, he never thought that he could earn an adequate living in the field.

When he left theology school, Bill returned home to Denver and worked briefly as an apprentice embalmer before finding a municipal financing job with the City of Denver. His supervisor encouraged him to consider a career in city management.

Over the next 20 years, Bill worked as city manager for a number of cities, from small to larger, starting with Montclair, California; Scottsdale, Arizona; and Tacoma, Washington, and then for five years in Cincinnati, one of the largest U.S. municipalities with a city manager form of government.

Here is where a lifelong passion for animals and the outdoors produced its dividend. He was on a field trip with a good friend, the director of the Cincinnati Zoo, to collect snakes, salamanders, and other reptiles. His friend, who was also president of the American Association of Zoological Parks and Aquariums, told him that the Philadelphia Zoo was looking for a new director. He thought that Bill's dual credentials in management and the outdoors made him ideal for the job.

"I thought he was kidding when he submitted my name as a candidate. After several interviews in Philadelphia, I was hired. When I finally built up the courage to tell my wife about taking the job, she was hardly surprised. She was always waiting for me to tell her that I had run off and joined the circus. Our two sons had already finished college, so it seemed logical to go work for a zoo when I was 49 instead of waiting to do this type of work when I retired."

From his first day on the job, Bill started applying the lessons that he had learned in 20 years of municipal government. His primary goal was to make the zoo financially independent. He started by revamping the zoo's fiscal ties with Philadelphia. As a financial alternative he produced new sources of revenue. Zoo membership grew in 10 years from 7000 to 48,000.

The budget increased from $3 to $14 million, yet this was offset by growing revenues from entrance fees, membership, concessions, and endowments. He obtained additional funds by having the zoo named by the state of New Jersey to build and manage an aquarium across the Delaware River in Camden.

As Cincinnati's city manager, Bill supervised 14,000 municipal employees. By comparison the zoo is actually a small operation.

"You approach problems differently, but the management principles are the same. However, in a zoo, if you don't like animals you won't have a good time. When I left Cincinnati, I had just completed a book on municipal finance and in my dedication to my friend at the Cincinnati Zoo I wrote, 'He taught me to be 21 at 50.'"

———————◆———————

Points to Remember

► Today's professional gardeners are highly trained.

► This is also a field in which you must start from the bottom.

► Entrepreneurial opportunities are available in gardening.

► Farming attracts career changers.

► You can learn your specialty at school or on the job.

► Farming is filled with niche specialties.

► The environmental field needs career changers with varied skills

———————◆———————

CHAPTER 17

Communications and the Arts

CAREER OPPORTUNITIES IN WRITING AND JOURNALISM

If your goal is finding a newspaper, magazine, television, or radio journalism job, be prepared for an arduous employment route. Most midsized to large news organizations hire only seasoned reporters and editors. Job opportunities are rather limited with the major media, and the competition is keen. A high turnover rate, however, creates openings.

Print and broadcast journalism are fields in which you are expected to "pay your dues," regardless of past careers and previous experience. Ignore the stories you've heard of a drama teacher who is hired as a theater critic or the investment banker who is a new financial columnist.

Compared with the daily press, trade and special interest publications recognize past experience. A jazz magazine hires writers who know jazz music, a medical magazine seeks health care professionals as reporters and editors, and computer publications pay a premium for writers who also know the bits and bytes of software programming.

An Ohio State University survey found the entry-level salaries in consumer print and broadcast media are comparable with the earnings of a new classroom teacher. In television journalism, says the Radio Television News Directors Association, the salaries of a handful of network anchors are very much the exception.

The typical local station anchor averages $50,000; producers, news editors and reporters earn proportionally less. In print journalism as recently as 1990, entry-level newspaper reporters earned about $18,000, compared with $13,000 in radio and $15,000 in television.

Writing seems to attract career changers, a number as mystery writers who integrate their past work into their books. Dick Francis, a one-time jockey, uses his knowledge of horses in books with a racing theme, and Robin Cook is a physician who writes medical thrillers.

THE CAREER SWITCHERS

Tom Clancy Finds Writing Beats Selling Insurance

If it wasn't for a specialty publisher, Tom Clancy (midforties) might still be selling insurance in Owings, Maryland. Unlike so many career changers, Clancy's motivation was not one of attempting to escape from the corporate world, nor was he an expert on the armed services, a basic theme in many of his books.

He already owned his own insurance agency, so his job and financial future were secure. Clancy wanted to be a writer, however, but he was sidetracked.

Writing became a more important part of his life in the early 1980s. His children were very young, and his wife would actually have been happier if he concentrated on selling insurance since it paid the family bills. But he was chasing a dream, one that had been further frustrated by a collection of magazine publishers' rejection slips. With little formal science education and no military training, he violated a cardinal principle: write about subjects you know.

Unlike John LeCarré, whose insight into espionage is based on personal experience in the British secret service, Clancy derives his expertise from imagination and exhaustive research. Fascinated with the military as a youngster, his poor eyesight prevented a career in the armed forces, and as a substitute, he became an avid reader of military books and journals.

Clancy submitted a magazine article on the MX missile system that was published by the U.S. Naval Institute's *Proceedings*. This encouraged him to research the technology of nuclear-powered submarines, information that was accessible in off-the-shelf naval journals and reference books.

Stealing time from the insurance business, it took Clancy 12 months to write *The Hunt for Red October*, which he submitted to the Naval Institute. They asked him to rewrite the book. The rest is history.

"Even if the book had not been successsful, I would have continued to write," he told *Nation's Business*. "My motive was not to make large amounts of money but rather to pay the bills, and even more to the point, pursue the dream to be a writer, a dream that dates back to high school."

Having Been a Judge Helps This TV Newscaster

When Catherine Crier (midthirties) was a youngster, she knew that she wanted to be a lawyer; her hero was trial lawyer Clarence Darrow.

Until 1989, there was little indication of a possible career change. Catherine was dedicated to law: Southern Methodist University School of Law, three years as an assistant district attorney, and several years as a practicing attorney. In 1984, she was elected a Texas state district judge, the youngest person to be elected a judge in the state's history.

"Shortly after being elected in 1988 to a second term, I met an independent TV producer who at one time headed recruiting for CBS News. We talked about politics and international affairs, two subjects near and dear to me. He asked me if I was interested in doing a political issue show. I was intrigued, and I made a sample interview tape that was sent to the networks. Several news organizations responded, including Cable Network News. Until then, I did not expect the project to come to fruition, and if it did, I assumed it could be done in conjunction with my regular judicial duties. I knew that I wanted to complete my second term on the bench and then move to something else but definitely in the law."

Catherine instead went to work for CNN in October 1989, and to her surprise she found a number of similarities between law and journalism. She left CNN to join ABC News in early 1993.

Most people see her changeover as a tremendous leap, but if you stop looking at job titles and instead look at substance, both fields have a lot in common. As a DA, she hit the streets, worked with police, interviewed witnesses, and put together a "story." It was not delivered to an editor but rather to a judge in the form of a pleading or a brief.

Although she didn't do a TV "stand-up" before a courthouse, Catherine did make final arguments in front of a jury. The elements of investigative reporting are the sorts of things that are incorporated into a trial lawyer's career. Like an impartial editor, a judge listens to both sides of an argument, evaluates and determines the facts, and attempts to understand the broader perspective.

What she had to learn was the fundamentals of TV broadcasting: how to use a teleprompter and how to effectively deliver the news.

Software Expert Turns to Journalism

Jeffrey Fox's (early forties) resume is hardly representative of the career of a magazine journalist. Until his changeover, he was a software engineer and entrepreneur. From the time he graduated from the State University of New York as an engineer, Jeff worked as a programmer with Citibank and several software design firms.

Interested in the relationship between computers and corporate management, he took a year off to get a master of information science degree at the Harvard University Business School.

The timing coincided perfectly with the introduction of microcomputer software in the early 1980s. As a software specialist in a new technical discipline, Jeff saw the potential business opportunities and founded Fox & Geller. It rapidly became a multimillion dollar software producer and was listed among the top 100 largest personal computer software companies.

"By 1988 I was tiring of business. We employed 30 people, and I didn't like some of the directions the company was taking. Business was no longer fun. I had an opportunity to get out, and I did. I didn't know what I would do, but I was determined not to work for someone else."

He did not rush into any new ventures. Without career objectives, Jeff wandered about New York at loose ends, and to escape he made a 10-week cross-country bike trip. Jeff was now married, however, and had family responsibilities. It was time to come home and make plans.

Jeff changed gears. Over the next six months, he executed a personal marketing plan to stimulate possible business leads and broaden his knowledge of a possible new career.

Considering the possibilities of buying a business, he placed ads in the *New York Times* and *Wall Street Journal*. As another career option, he mailed hundreds of letters to potential employers, purchased career books, went to a career counselor, and attended New York University's midlife career-counseling course.

During a coast-to-coast bike trip the seeds of a journalism career were sown. It was perhaps a throwback to a boyhood hobby. When he was 11, Jeff and a friend wrote and printed a one-page homemade newspaper.

With his computer industry skills, his search would have ended if he wanted a job on a computer industry trade publication or if he decided to start his own software newsletter. After nearly 20 years in computers, Jeff wanted to break away from computers.

It was time to get to work. Step one, professional training, was obtained at the Columbia University Graduate School of Journalism. Step two was finding a job in a tight employment market. The search ended in January 1990, when he replied to a *Consumer Reports* classified ad for a staff writer.

Jeff's computer and business skills enabled him to get the job. Like the other finalists, he was given a trial assignment, and instead of treating it routinely, he added a creative touch.

Using his desktop computer, he wrote and then printed a several-page story so it would appear identical in style and format to a *Consumer Reports* article. Fortunately, he had as a guide copies of the magazine, which he had saved for the past 10 years.

Although no longer a programmer or corporate executive, Jeff thinks like a hybrid journalist-engineer. When he interviews technicians, he talks their language and has the professional know-how to make accurate interpretations and evaluations of their technical findings.

CAREER OPPORTUNITIES IN PUBLIC RELATIONS

The public relations field welcomes skilled career changers. Employers buy carry-forward skills, since public relations blends a number of capabilities: oral and written presentations, sales expertise, and media knowledge. Previous business and professional experience, as well as related academic training, is a decided employment advantage in public relations agencies and corporate, nonprofit, or governmental public relations departments.

The entry-level salary for a recent college graduate might range between $18,000 and $23,000, but salaries for career changers are based on the other capabilities that are brought to the table. Public relations is also a field in which 60 percent of the professionals are women, says the Jack O'Dwyer News Letter.

Keen competition is likely to continue in the pubic relations job market. According to the U.S. Bureau of Labor Statistics, the vast majority of job opportunities will result from the need to replace specialists who leave the field. In addition, opportunities will occur in corporations and organizations of all sizes that recognize the need for good internal and external communications.

THE CAREER SWITCHERS

Army Know-how Creates a Civilian Job

Stephen Naru (midthirties) intended to make the army his career until he was stonewalled. He then had to move quickly and make alternative plans.

Graduating third in his high school class and as an all-state Michigan halfback, Steve attended West Point, placed first in his class in history, and upon graduation was sent to Germany for nearly five years with the Air Defense Command.

When he completed his overseas tour, Steve was assigned to West Point's admissions office as a public relations officer. Before the transfer, the Army sent him to Michigan State University to earn a journalism degree and obtain skills that would be useful in his upcoming assignment.

His new assignment was ideally suited to his wife, Barbara, a nurse, who found it easier to find hospital employment in an upstate New York hospital than in Germany. Steve was responsible for managing and implementing West Point's public relations and marketing program to attract future cadets. He supervised the planning, writing, editing, and design of over 200 promotional publications, never realizing that he was also building value-added credentials that would provide an entrée to another career.

After four years at West Point, he was notified that he was placed on the promotion list to major, meaning that he would also be eligible to attend the Command and General Staff School the following year.

In keeping with standard military policy, Steve would be assigned to another military base for one year before going to school. Steve requested permission to spend a fifth year at West Point before his transfer. It would mean one less move for his family and less pressure on Barbara, who was now a nursing supervisor at a local hospital. The Army proved to be inflexible. Regulations, he was told, could not be altered.

Until then, Steve expected to make the Army his career; public relations was not part of his long-term military goal. He looked forward to returning to a field command.

The Army's lack of flexibility rapidly changed Steve's plans. A friend sent his resumé to Burson-Marsteller in New York City, which represented the Army's Recruitment Service and the Postal Service, public relations clients that could benefit from his experience.

A job was offered, and Steve resigned his commission in May 1989, almost 14 years after he entered West Point as a cadet. Three days later he went to work for Burson-Marsteller.

"It was on-the-job adjustment to civilian public relations. Things differed; it was easy selling a story idea at West Point. The press came to me. The situation was now reversed. I had to go out and sell a story. I learned this is the real world." A year after he joined the firm, Steve was made a vice president and subsequently a senior vice president and has more than doubled his military salary.

From PR to Restaurants and Back to PR

Alfred Geduldig's (midfifties) career has come full circle. His travels have taken him from corporate public relations to restaurant ownership and back to public relations.

Al attended the Cornell University School of Hotel Management, but he never completed the course. After graduating from New York University, he worked in corporate communications for the Ford Foundation and Mobil Oil Corporation and as a vice president of GAF Corporation (now International Specialty Products, Inc.).

Even though he was pleased with his rapid corporate advancement, Al was dissatisfied with the intangible aspects of public relations. He always liked the restaurant business despite his aborted Cornell education.

Compared with PR, restaurants now seemed a more creative way to earn a living. Al also turned 41, and he was beginning to think in terms of his mortality; he wanted to be remembered for more than a career in public relations.

He left New York and moved to Charleston, Rhode Island, a resort town, where he owned a summer home. He bought Windswept Farms, and on the property he created a three-restaurant complex plus an antique store and movie theater. Whenever possible, he applied his communications know-how to promote this business.

One restaurant featured authentic colonial foods, which Al promoted with a menu in the format of a newspaper of the period. The second restaurant, which became the hub of the complex, specialized in hamburgers and chili, and as one would expect in New England, the third restaurant featured fish and seafood.

"Little did I know that when I opened in 1978, we would be in the midst of an oil crisis. People weren't traveling. Tourism, an important part of my business plan, fell 30 percent below expectation. Gas was in short supply, and prices were high. I also discovered that the colonial inn had a fundamental marketing flaw. Customers liked the historical theme but they came once and never returned."

Al had already invested about $1.5 million in the project. To cut his losses, he converted the colonial inn to the Wooden Nickel, which specialized in steak and duck.

"During the five years we were in business I never took a salary, but at least my wife and children had food to eat." When applicable, Al used his PR know-how to attract customers. During February, the slowest part of his year-round operation, he featured an aphrodisiac menu on Valentine's Day. His menu of champagne, chocolate coffee, oysters, and other delicacies resulted in a half-page story in the *Providence Journal*, the state's leading daily newspaper.

With business still sluggish, Al decided to return to public relations. He sent out resumes, and in response, he was offered a job as vice president of corporate communications at the Travelers Companies.

Three years later, he left Travelers to start a consulting firm that advises corporate public relations departments, illustrating once again "what goes around, comes around."

Al paid a price for his five years of restaurant ownership. He took only two days of vacation, worked 16 hours a day, and depleted his savings. Nearly eight years after closing Windswept Farms, Al is still paying off the balance of the debt.

CAREER OPPORTUNITIES IN ART AND ACTING

The artists and actors profiled in *It's Never Too Late* have similar backgrounds: all but one is a college graduate, several have doctorates, and, most significantly, they all learned their new trade on the job. Since they were employed as they made their career changeover, they developed and perfected their skills as part-timers.

Several supplemented on-the-job training by attending professional institutes or with a private coach. When they built confidence, some professional credits, and the all-important financial reserves, they were ready to make a full-time commitment. Even so, several continue to work part-time to help pay the bills.

THE CAREER SWITCHERS

Nuclear Physicist Turns Cartoonist

Robert Sutton Grace, better known as Bud Grace, is approximately 40. He avoids giving his precise age or providing chronological references, a pattern somewhat consistent with the whimsical characters in his syndicated cartoon, "Ernie." Professionally, Bud is a nuclear physicist with a PhD from Florida State University.

"I was never really excited about the field, but I was good in math and physics. Physics, however, was more fun than math so I went in that direction."

Over the next few years, Bud taught at the University of Georgia, was a postdoctoral fellow at Florida State, and during the oil crisis worked as an energy administrator. Offered another teaching post at Florida State, he decided that he really was no longer interested in working in science, but he was undecided about what he really wanted to do. "What I really wanted to do was draw and write. There was a problem. I didn't know how to draw."

He spent the next six years developing an art style while teaching science part-time in the Washington, D.C. area. "I never took an art or cartoon lesson. I developed my own style. I took to cartooning because fine art was more complex and I knew that I could never make a living from it. Little did I realize the difficulty in good cartooning."

By the mid-1980s, Bud was submitting cartoon strips to publishers and syndicates, and like many other hopeful cartoonists, all he collected was rejection slips. Finally, the portfolio sent to King Features hit pay dirt.

In 1988, the adventures of working class people and the central character, Ernie, who manages a fast-food restaurant that sells squid burgers, was officially born and syndicated. The strip is the creation of Bud's personality.

None of his characters are based on composites of friends or family, and only occasionally does he use science as a theme of a strip. After a trial run, a few newspapers dropped "Ernie," claiming it was vulgar or sexist. Despite earlier protests, the strip gained increased support in readership surveys and is syndicated in several hundred U.S. newspapers and in Japan, India, and Europe.

Contrary to popular belief about the creativity process, few if any of the ideas or humor in "Ernie" result from leisure time inspiration.

"I work at ideas, since I'm not clever at thinking of things to say. I spend 50 to 60 hours a week in my studio. On a good day, I might complete three strips. Nearly all the humor comes from inside. My job is to create something out of nothing; I'm actually in the business of manufacturing cartoons."

From Letterpress to Graphic Brick Walls

James Marshall (early fifties) is Canada's only carver of bricks and one of the few specialists in this craft in North America. As a youngster, he created his own comic book story about a World War II bomber crew, "The Lost Squadron," and also designed posters for his father's linotype and letterpress printing shop in Medicine Hat, Alberta.

Raised as a printer, he went to Toronto to study the trade and while there he discovered what was then a new technique, offset printing. No sooner had Jim returned to Medicine Hat than he convinced his father to convert to offset production; lithography was just starting to take hold in Alberta in the late 1950s.

"Within a few years, we did nothing but offset printing. But I was not satisfied with the direction my career was taking. I actually was intrigued with the idea of working for a large company."

Jim was hired as public relations and advertising representative by I-XL Industries, Ltd., a Canadian company that markets a line of bricks. At architectural trade shows, his job was to demonstrate the use of brick in home and public building decor, and he saw the potential of turning an industrial product into an art form.

He and his wife Lorine, a textile artist, as partners started Grassroots Studios, and several years later, convinced that there was a market for artistic brick walls, he left I-XL Industries.

The process of brick carving starts with a set of precise drawings and then moves to scaled blueprints and finally to carved bricks. Large panels of green bricks are swaddled in plastic to retain their moisture. At this time, Marshall carves the story. It is not unusual for him to work upward of 80 hours a week. Carved panels are then dismantled, dried for up to six weeks, fired, and then assembled on-site.

Working at first as a pen-and-ink artist to produce income, he began to receive assignments to create carved brick walls. In 1983, Jim received a commission to create two 9- by 18-foot panels depicting the legend behind Medicine Hat's colorful name and a series of panels depicting the 14 stations of the cross for the Roman Catholic Church in Toronto.

"Being an artist is a tough way to make a living. You seldom reach the point in your lifetime where your work brings in enough money so you're consistently earning large fees."

The price of his work fluctuates like the price of real estate, but he normally charges about $100 a square foot of artwork. Jim particularly enjoys his lifestyle, one that brings together his sales and artistic skills and living in western Canada.

The Realtor Carves Fish

Fritz Ralph (late forties) wasn't always a craftsman. After graduating from college in California, he worked for 17 years for Carrier Corporation, a company that had also employed his father. By the time he left Carrier in the late 1970s, Fritz was comptroller of the company's West Coast operation.

Seeking new challenges, he left Carrier, moved to Bakersfield, and got a job selling commercial real estate. When Fritz left Carrier, his wife, Elaine, went to work for a doctor since he wasn't confident that he'd make a sufficient income as a salesman. Elaine developed a management system for the doctor, which she then sold to other doctors.

Fritz was born in upstate New York but he left there when his father was transferred by Carrier to California. By the mid-1980s, his mother, now living near Syracuse, New York, was in bad health.

"Elaine's parents had both died several years earlier, and like a lot of people, we suddenly realized how important it is to have your parents around. By that time, we had also tired of the cement, the crowds, and the pace of California life. When we came East, I had no clear idea of how I was going to make a living."

Fritz wanted to be self-employed, perhaps in the mail-order business or doing something related to the environment. Both Ralphs enjoy the outdoors and are ardent naturalists.

Searching for ideas, they attended a crafts show in New York City, and after looking at more than 1000 exhibits, Fritz was impressed by a craftsman who machine-carved replicas of decoys. What particularly impressed him was that the craftsman's line was sold out a year in advance. He saw a potential market demand for fish carved out of wood.

Fritz had not yet demonstrated any artistic talent. His art education began by studying books on wood carving. He soon discovered the natural wood carvings of fish were not very attractive. He recruited Elaine to paint the fish while he concentrated on carving. At first, they worked up to 14 hours a day, seven days a week learning their trade.

Five months later "Smiley," a large mouth bass, won "best in class" in a regional carving contest and they were in business. Within a year, they reached the point at which their lifelike painted wood carvings sold for $2500 or more and they had a two-year backlog on orders.

There's No Business Like Show Business

Wallace Sheretz's (midfifties) career goal to be an actor was sidetracked for more than 20 years. He graduated from college after serving two years in the U.S. Marine Corps and working for six years as a draftsman.

He worked as a classroom teacher in Texas and Colorado for eight years. Wallace realized that there is more money in administration than teaching. Since his father was an AFL/CIO member, it was only natural to become involved in the union movement and at the same time a good way to serve education.

While teaching in Colorado, he negotiated the state's first comprehensive agreement between teachers and a school district. His work in Colorado did not go unnoticed. He received a number of awards, including an "Outstanding Young Men of America" award from the Junior Chamber of Commerce and an Outstanding Service to Education award in Jefferson County, Colorado the following year.

After serving as a labor negotiator with the Colorado Education Association, Wallace moved East to join the Virginia Professional Staff Association and he renewed his long-standing interest in the theater.

"About 1980, I started performing as an actor and singer in amateur summer stock and community theater. Until then, I had no formal training; amateur productions were a good way to gain experience. Five years later, I gave up my full-time job as a labor negotiator and moved to New York." By then, family expenses were lower since his children were on their own. Even so, within the first year he used nearly all his savings on private acting lessons.

Over the next 10 years, Wallace has built impressive theatrical credentials: performing on afternoon TV soaps and commercials; off-Broadway, regional stock and national tour theater singing Tevye in *Fiddler on the Roof* and Merlin in *Camelot*; and playing the lead part in *Our Town*. To perform these different roles,

Wallace has developed New England, English, French, East European, Italian, Southern, German, and Irish stage accents.

Teaching proved to be good training for an actor. "Although I never used the classroom as a stage, teaching taught me how to be organized and to work hard."

Even with an impressive portfolio, steady work is difficult to find in today's lean theatrical market. It's a buyer's market, in which even household names rarely know when they'll receive their next acting job. To pay household expenses, Wallace works as a paralegal secretary.

The Life of a Stand-up Comedian

Paul Jacobs (midfifties) belongs to a diverse group of organizations: the American Educational Research Association, the Authors Guild, and the Professional Comedians Association. Strange as it seems, the memberships actually reflect Paul's different careers.

"My career change started when my biologic clock began to wind down. It was now or never. My decision to trade in a tenured job for the uncertain life of a stand-up comedian was made easier since I had few day-to-day personal responsibilities." His children had their own careers.

Like other performers, Paul has hedged his bets during the changeover to a new career. He works as an independent educational consultant for several New Jersey school districts. Until he decided on a career as a comedian, Paul, who has a doctorate in experimental psychology, spent approximately 30 years as a college educator and in educational research.

In high school and college, he was not involved in amateur theatrical groups, nor was he the family comedian. As a teacher, Paul injected humor into his lectures when he found that a lighter touch attracted more student interest.

In 1973, he took his first professional stab as a stand-up comic when he was between jobs. Club Therapy in New York City was looking for a comedian with a psychology routine. Paul answered its classified ad and got the Saturday night job, which paid $25 plus a free dinner for two.

The same day that he was interviewed, Paul was hired by the National Nursing League as a staff researcher. The job didn't start for three months. He performed several nights at Club Therapy, became ill, and by the time he was ready to return to work the club had folded. Paul resigned his college job 17 years later to concentrate on his comedy routine.

Paul does not want to be stereotyped as a comedian with a psychology routine, yet he applies his academic training and research skills in preparing his act.

"Before a club date, I visit the club, see others perform, and try to read the audience. This is important, since I write my own routines and then work from the memorized script. I rehearse by first taping my act with a video camera and then reviewing it. One thing I avoid is letting friends and family critique my act. They're rarely objective."

Points to Remember

► It's hard to find entry-level jobs on big city media.

► Specialized media look for writers with specialty skills.

► You need to start at the bottom in media jobs.

► Past business and professional experience is often useful in finding a job.

► The public relations field is expanding.

► Past skills are highly useful in getting PR jobs.

► Show business requires a second job to pay the bills.

Notes

CHAPTER 1

1. "Gaining New Perspectives on Medicine," *New York Times* (September 9, 1990), D-19.
2. *Encouraging Employee Self-Management in Financial and Career Planning* (New York: The Conference Board, 1991).
3. *Sports Illustrated* (April 17, 1989), p. 88.
4. Daniel Levinson, *The Seasons of a Man's Life* (New York: Alfred A. Knopf, 1978), p. 20.
5. Michael Maccoby, *The Gamesman* (New York: Simon & Shuster, 1976), p. 46–49.
6. Richard Ford, *The Sportswriter* (New York: Vintage Press, 1986), p. 7.

CHAPTER 2

1. "After the Fall," *Wall Street Journal* (August 24, 1992), p. A-1.
2. "The New Low-Risk Entrepreneurs," *Fortune Magazine* (July 27, 1992), p. 84.

CHAPTER 3

1. *First There Was a Dream* (San Francisco: Frederick Gilbert Associates, 1984), p. 1.
2. "Illegal Procedure, He's Heard of That," *New York Times* (February 2, 1991), p. B-4.
3. "Potter's Touch," *New Physician* (July–August 1990), p. 44.
4. "Doubling up on the Degrees," *U.S. News & World Reports* (October 22, 1990), p. 80.
5. "The Midlife Ministers," *Washington Post* (April 12, 1992), p. F1.

CHAPTER 4

1. Carol Aslanian and Henry Brickell, *How Americans in Transition Study for College Credits* (New York: Conference Board, 1988).
2. "About New York," *New York Times* (May 4, 1991), p. 27.

CHAPTER 5

1. "The Doctor's World," *New York Times* (September 3, 1991), p. C-3.

CHAPTER 6

1. Witold Rybcynski, *Waiting for the Weekend* (New York: Viking, 1991), p. 142.
2. *Redefining Corporate Sabbaticals for the 1990s* (New York: Conference Board, 1992).
3. "Executive Life," *Fortune Magazine* (May 27, 1989), p. 80.
4. "Executive Life," *New York Times* (June 3, 1990), p. B-25.
5. "A Broadcaster Who's Now a Home-Based CEO," *Home Office Computing* (June 1991), p. 43.

CHAPTER 7

1. "The Fourth Alternative: Leisure Search and Planning," *Journal of Employment Counseling* (June 1991), p. 57.
2. Personal interview and *Hermes*, Columbia University Graduate School of Business (Summer 1989), p. 37.

CHAPTER 8

1. "Heroes for Hire," *U.S. News & World Report* (February 17, 1992), p. 16.
2. "When Johnny Comes Marching Home Again," *Industry Week* (August 17, 1992), p. 14.
3. "From the Armed Forces to the Teaching Forces, *Wall Street Journal* (January 10, 1992), p. A-8.

CHAPTER 9

1. Helen Freidus, "The Call of the Sirens? The Influence of Gender in the Decision to Choose Teaching as a Second Career." Paper presented at the American Educational Research Association annual meeting, April 1990.
2. National Center for Education Information, 1990.
3. Personal interview and "From Corporation to Classroom," *Instructor* (October 1990), p. 35.

Bibliography

Arron, Deborah L., 1989. *Running from the Law* (Seattle: Niche Press).

Aslanian, Carol, and Brickell, Henry, 1988. *How Americans in Transition Study for College Credit* (New York: College Board).

Bolles, Richard Nelson, 1981. *The Three Boxes of Life* (Berkeley, CA: Ten Speed Press).

Bolles, Richard Nelson, 1991. *What Color Is Your Parachute?* (Berkeley, CA: Ten Speed Press).

Brans, Jo, 1989. *Take Two* (New York: Doubleday).

Cotham, James C., III, 1988. *Career Shock* (New York: Donald I. Fine).

Dychtwald, Ken, 1990. *Age Wave* (New York: Bantam Books).

Handy, Charles, 1990. *The Age of Unreason* (London: Arrow Books).

Hawes, Gene W., 1985. *The Encyclopedia of Second Careers* (New York: Facts on File, Inc.).

Hennig, Margaret, and Jardim, Anne, 1977. *The Managerial Woman* (New York: Pocket Books).

Hyatt, Carole, 1990. *Shifting Gears* (New York: Simon & Schuster).

Jones, Rochelle, 1980. *The Big Switch* (New York: McGraw-Hill).

Levinson, Daniel J., 1978. *The Seasons of a Man's Life* (New York: Ballantine Books).

Rybcynski, Witold, 1991. *Waiting for the Weekend* (New York: Viking).

Saltzman, Amy, 1990. *Downsizing* (New York: HarperCollins).

Sheehy, Gail, 1976. *Passages* (New York: Bantam Books).

Sheehy, Gail, 1981. *Pathfinders* (New York: William Morrow).

Snelling, Robert O., Sr. and Snelling, Anne M., 1992. *Jobs* (New York: Fireside, Simon & Schuster).

Sonnenfeld, Jeffrey, 1988. *The Hero's Farewell* (New York: Oxford University Press).

Terhorst, Paul, 1988. *Cashing in the American Dream...How to Retire at 35* (New York: Bantam Books).

U.S. Department of Labor. *Occupational Handbook*, 1992–93. (Washington, DC).

Waterman, Robert H., Jr., 1988. *The Renewal Factor* (New York: Bantam Books).

Resources

This section provides the names of key *national* organizations and publications to contact for information on a specific career or field of interest.

For additional information, the reference rooms of most mid-sized and large libraries have other directories available.

The Encyclopedia of Associations lists over 23,000 national and international organizations.

Bacon's Publicity Checker lists more than 9200 business, trade, industrial, professional, and consumer publications.

In addition, the general news and business media, such as *Time Magazine, Newsweek,* the *Wall Street Journal, Fortune Magazine, Business Week, U.S. News & World Report, Working Woman* and *U.S.A. Today,* along with large metropolitan dailies, publish articles on career trends on a regular basis.

National Business Employment Weekly specializes in covering careers and employment opportunities. *American Demographics* regularly publishes career-related articles.

These publications can be purchased on newstands; those listed later are normally found in larger public libraries and university and professional libraries or by subscription from the publisher.

Entrepreneurs should use the small business administration office in their community and the local chamber of commerce as a source of valuable business information.

CHAPTER 9: EDUCATION

Start your search at a college-level school or department of education. Information on regular and alternative teacher certification is available from the department of education teacher training and certification office (or an equivalent title) in each state.

Contact

American Association of Colleges for Teacher Education, 1 Dupont Circle, Washington, DC 20036; (202)293-2450.

American Association of University Professors, 1012 14th Street, NW, Washington, DC 20005; (202)737-5900.

American Federation of Teachers, 555 New Jersey Avenue, NW, Washington, DC 20001; (202)879-4400.

National Association of Independent Schools, 75 Federal Street, Boston, MA 02110; (617)451-2444.

National Catholic Education Association, 1077 30th Street, NW, Washington, DC 20007; (202)337-6232.

National Council for Accreditation of Teacher Education, 2010 Massachusetts Avenue, Washington, DC 20036; (202)466-7496.

National Education Association, 1201 16th Street, NW, Washington, DC 20036; (202)833-4000.

National Executive Service Corps, 257 Park Avenue South, New York, NY 10010; (212)529-6660.

U.S. Department of Education, Office of Public Affairs, 400 Maryland Avenue, SW, Washington, DC 20202; (202)732-4564.

Read

Chronicle of Higher Education, 1255 23d Street, NW, Washington, DC 20037; (202) 466-1000.

Education Week, 4301 Connecticut Avenue, NW, Washington, DC 20008; (202)364-4114.

NEA Today, 1201 16th Street, NW, Washington, DC 20036; (202)822-7200.

CHAPTER 10: HEALTH CARE

Medicine

If medicine is your goal, start your search by investigating local colleges and universities that offer postbaccalaureate premedical programs. There's no harm, either, in visiting the admission offices of a few medical schools. They can provide the names of the good predoc programs in your area, as well as a briefing on their own admissions policy. Some even give the names of other career changers who are attending or have completed medical training. State and local medical societies maintain reference libraries.

Contact

American Medical Association, 515 North State Street, Chicago, IL 60610; (312)464-5000.

American Medical Woman's Association, 801 North Fairfax Street, Alexandria, VA 22209; (703)838-0500.

American Osteopathic Association, 142 East Ontario Street, Chicago, IL 60611; (312)280-5800.

Association of American Medical Colleges, 2450 N Street, NW, Washington, DC 20037; (202)828-0400.

Read

Medical Economics, 5 Paragon Drive, Montvale, NJ 07645; (201)358-7500.

Medical Tribune, 257 Park Avenue South, New York, NY 10016; (212)674-8500.

New Physician, 1890 Preston White Drive, Reston, VA 22091; (703)620-6600.

Nursing

Candidates should research a nursing career in a similar way as to those considering medicine.

Contact

American Association of Colleges of Nursing, One Dupont Circle, NW, Washington, DC 20036; (202)463-6930.

American Health Care Association, 1201 L Street, NW, Washington, DC 20005; (202)842-4444.

American Nursing Association, 600 Maryland Avenue, SW, Washington, DC 20024; (202)554-4444.

National League for Nursing, 350 Hudson Street, New York, NY 10014; (212)989-9393.

National Student Nurses Association, 555 West 57th Street, New York, NY 10019; (212)581-2211.

Read

American Journal of Nursing, 555 West 57th Street, New York, NY 10019; (212)582-8820.

American Nurse, 600 Maryland Avenue, SW, Washington, DC 20024; (202)554-4444.

Nursing World Journal, 470 Boston Post Road, Weston, MA 02193; (617)889-2702.

RN, 5 Paragon Drive, Montvale, NJ 07645; (201)358-7500.

CHAPTER 11: LAW

Speak to lawyer friends, attend a law school open house, read law school catalogs and literature, and visit the offices of the state and county bar associations.

Contact

American Bar Association, 750 North Lake Shore Drive, Chicago, IL 60611; (312)988-5000.

Association of American Law Schools, 1201 Connecticut Avenue, NW, Washington, DC 20036; (202)296-8851.

Law School Admission Services, Box 40, Newtown, PA 18904; (215)968-1101.

National Association of Law Placement, 1666 Connecticut Avenue, NW, Washington, DC 20006; (202)667-1666.

Read

ABA Journal, 750 North Lake Shore Drive, Chicago, IL 60611; (312)988-5000.

American Lawyer, 600 Third Avenue, New York, NY 10016; (212)973-2800.

National Law Journal, 111 Eighth Avenue, New York, NY 10011; (212)741-8300.

CHAPTER 12: CLERGY

For all faiths, the logical starting point is the applicant's own religious advisor and other members of the clergy in your community.

Contact

Protestant

The National Council of Churches of Christ in the USA, 475 Riverside Drive, New York, NY 10115; (212)870-2227 (the Council serves as a central clearinghouse for a number of different Protestant denominations).

(Baptist) Southern Baptist Convention, 901 Commerce Street, Nashville, TN 37203; (615)244-2355.

(Eastern Orthodox) Greek Orthodox Archdiocese of North and South America, 8 East 79th Street, New York, NY 10021; (212)570-3500.

(Episcopal) Episcopal Church, 815 Second Avenue, New York, NY 10017; (212)867-8400.

(Lutheran) Evangelical Lutheran Church in America, 8765 West Higgins Road, Chicago, IL 60631; (313)380-2700.

Lutheran Church Missouri Synod, 1333 South Kirkwood, St. Louis, MO; (314)965-9000.

(Methodist) United Methodist Church, 475 Riverside Drive, New York, NY 10027; (212)870-3600.

(Mormon) Church of Jesus Christ of Latter-Day Saints, 50 East North Temple Street, Salt Lake City, UT 84150; (801)240-1000.

(Presbyterian) Presbyterian Church (USA), 100 Witherspoon Street, Louisville, KY 40202; (502)569-5000.

(Reformed) United Church of Christ, 700 Prospect Avenue, East Cleveland, OH 44115; (215)736-2121.

Roman Catholic

National Conference of Catholic Bishops, 3211 Fourth Street, NE, Washington, DC 20017; (202)541-3000.

National Conference of Diocesan Vocation Directors, 1603 South Michigan Avenue, Chicago, IL 60616; (312)663-5456.

Jewish

(Reform) Union of American Hebrew Congregations, 838 Fifth Avenue, New York, NY 10021; (212)249-0100.

(Conservative) United Synagogue of America, 155 Fifth Avenue, New York, NY 10010; (212)533-7800.

(Orthodox) Union of Orthodox Jewish Congregations of America, 45 West 36th Street, New York, NY 10018; (212)563-4000.

Read

Catholic Digest, 2115 Summit Avenue, St. Paul, MN 55105; (612)647-5296.

Christianity Today, 465 Gunderson Drive, Carol Stream, IL 60188; (708)260-6200.

CHAPTER 13:
COMMUNITY SERVICE AND PSYCHOLOGY

Contact

American Psychological Association, 750 First Street, NE, Washington, DC 20002; (202)336-5500.

Council on Social Work Education, 1600 Duke Street, Alexandria, VA 22314; (703)683-8080.

National Association of Social Workers, 750 First Street, NE, Washington, DC 20002; (202)408-8600.

Read

American Psychologist, 750 First Street, NE, Washington, DC 20002; (202)336-5500.
Social Work, 750 First Street, NE, Washington, DC 20002; (202)408-8600.

CHAPTER 14:
RETAIL AND SERVICE BUSINESSES

Bookselling
Contact

American Booksellers Association, 560 White Plains Road, Tarrytown, NY 10591; (914)631-7800.

Read

Publisher's Weekly, 249 West 17th Street, New York, NY 10011; (212)463-6752.

Bed-and-Breakfast Inns
Contact

American Bed and Breakfast Association, 1407 Huguenot Road, Midlothian, VA 23113; (804)379-2222.
National Bed and Breakfast Association, Box 332, Norwalk, CT 06852; (203)847-6196.

Read

Inn Business Review, 105 East Court Street, Kankakee, IL 60901; (815)939-3509.
Innkeeping World, Box 84108, Seattle, WA 98124; (206)362-7125.

Food and Restaurants
Contact

American Culinary Federation, Box 3466, St. Augustine, FL 32085; (904)824-4468.
Chefs de Cuisine Association of America, 50 Hidden Glen Road, Upper Saddle River, NJ 07458; (201)825-8455.

Read

Nation's Restaurant News, 425 Park Avenue, New York, NY 10022;
(212)756-5200.
Restaurant Business, 633 Third Avenue, New York, NY 10017;
(212)986-4800.

CHAPTER 15: GARDENING, FARMING, AND THE ENVIRONMENT

Gardening

Contact

American Association of Botanical Gardens and Arboreta, 786
Church Road, Wayne, PA 19087; (215)688-1120.

Read

American Horticulturist, 7931 East Boulevard Drive, Alexandria,
VA 22308; (703)768-5700.
Landscape Management, 7500 Old Oak Boulevard, Cleveland, OH
44130; (216)242-8100.

Farming

County extension service offices are located in nearly every county
in the United States.

Contact

American Farm Bureau Federation, 225 Touhy Avenue, Park
Ridge, IL 60068; (312)399-5700.
American Society of Farm Managers and Appraisers, 950 South
Cherry Street, Denver, CO 80222; (303)758-3513.

Read

Agweek, 113 North 3rd Street, Grand Forks, ND 58206;
(701)780-1230.
Successful Farming, 1716 Locust Street, Des Moines, IO 50336;
(515)284-3000.

Environment

Contact

American Forestry Association, 1516 P Street, NW, Washington,
DC 20005; (202)667-3300.

National Audubon Society, 700 Broadway, New York, NY 10003; (212)979-3000.

Sierra Club, 730 Polk Street, San Francisco, CA 94109; (415)776-2211.

Read

Environment Today, 1165 North Chase Parkway, Marietta, GA 30067; (404)988-9558.

Environmental Science & Technology, 1155 16th Street, NW, Washington, DC 20036; (202)872-4600.

CHAPTER 16: HOME DECOR

Contact

American Crafts Council, 72 Spring Street, New York, NY 10012; (212)274-0630.

American Society of Interior Designers, 608 Massachusetts Avenue, NE, Washington, DC 20002; (202)546-3480.

Hobby Industry Association of America (HIA), 319 East 54th Street, Elmwood Park, NJ 07407; (201)794-1133.

Read

American Crafts, 72 Spring Street, New York, NY 10012; (212)274-0630.

American Woodworker, 33 East Minor Street, Emmaus, PA 18098; (215)967-5171.

Crafts, News Plaza, Box 1790, Peoria, IL 61656; (309)682-6626.

HFD, 7 East 12th Street, New York, NY 10003; (212)630-4800.

Interior Design, 245 West 17th Street, New York, NY 10011; (212)645-0067.

CHAPTER 17:
COMMUNICATIONS AND THE ARTS

Media

Contact

American Business Press, 675 Third Avenue, New York, NY 10017; (212)661-6360.

American Society of Newspaper Editors, 11600 Sunrise Valley Drive, Reston, VA 22091; (703)648-1144.

Magazine Publishers Association, 575 Lexington Avenue, New York, NY 10022; (212)752-0055.

National Association of Broadcasters, 1771 N Street, NW, Washington, DC 20036; (202)429-5300.

Newspaper Publishers Association, 11600 Sunrise Valley Drive, Reston, VA 22091; (703)648-1000.

Read

Broadcasting, 1705 DeSales Street, NW, Washington, DC 20036; (202)659-2340.

Editor & Publisher, 11 West 19th Street, New York, NY 10011; (212)675-4380.

Folio, 911 Hope Street, Stamford, CT 06907; (203)358-9900.

Writer's Digest, 1507 Dana Avenue, Cincinnati, OH 45207; (513)531-2222.

Public Relations

Contact

Public Relations Society of America, 33 Irving Place, New York, NY 10003; (212)995-2230.

International Association of Business Communicators, One Hallidie Plaza, San Francisco, CA 94102; (415)433-3400.

Read

Advertising Age, 220 East 42nd Street, New York, NY 10017; (212)210-0100.

Jack O'Dwyer's Newsletter, 271 Madison Avenue, New York, NY 10016; (212)679-2471.

Public Relations Journal, 33 Irving Place, New York, NY 10003; (212)995-2230.

Arts

Contact

Actor's Equity, 165 West 46 Street, New York, NY 10036; (212)869-8350.

Read

American Artists, 1515 Broadway, New York, NY 10036; (212)764-7300.

Variety, 475 Park Avenue South, New York, NY 10016; (212)779-1100.